DECORATIVE WREATHS & GARLANDS

DECORATIVE WREATHS & GARLANDS

20 BEAUTIFUL PROJECTS USING FLOWERS AND FABRICS

Hilary More and Pamela Westland

NORTH
LIGHT
BOOKS

CINCINNATI, OHIO

First published in Great Britain in 1994
by Anaya Publishers Ltd, London House,
Great Eastern Wharf, Parkgate Road, London SW11 4NQ

First published in North America
in 1995 by North Light Books,
an imprint of F&W Publications, Inc.
1507 Dana Avenue
Cincinnati, OH 45207
800/289-0963

Editor: Alison Wormleighton
Designer: Clare Clements
Photography: James Duncan
Styling: Madeleine Brehaut
Illustrations: Coral Mula

ISBN 0-89134-662-7

Typeset by Litho Link Ltd, Welshpool, Powys, Wales
Colour reproduction by J. Film Process, Singapore
Printed in Hong Kong by Dah Hua Printing Co Ltd

CONTENTS

INTRODUCTION

With the minimum of fuss and only a little knowledge of basic techniques, you can create a swag, wreath or garland to decorate your home or give as a gift. Each one is highly individual, so you can tailor it exactly to your decor or to the occasion.

Swags, garlands and wreaths have their origins deep in cultures all around the world, going right back to ancient times. The wreath symbolized love and friendship, welcome, protection, eternity and even life itself. Floral headdresses were worn by a bride and groom as a sign of purity, while circlets of the first flowers of spring were hung on doorways to bring good luck and deter evil spirits. Garlands of laurel and other evergreen leaves presented to the victors at ancient games and to conquering heroes returning from battle were proffered as a sign of honour. Ribbons of long-lasting flowers were draped across walls and furniture in homes and places of worship. Today, floral garlands spiralling around the poles of a marquee at a wedding reception and around church pillars at Easter and Christmas, and flower-decked swags hanging on either side of an arch or fireplace, are descendants of this practice.

Festoons of fruit and flowers, and graceful swags of fabric, were widely used in Classical ornament, as were garlands of flowers and foliage either draped in loops or with their ends joined to form wreaths. (A *swag* is either a horizontal festoon, which is suspended at each end and hangs in a curve in between, or a vertical cluster, which is suspended at the top. A *garland* is long and flexible enough to twine around things, while a garland with the ends joined is a *wreath*.)

From the earliest beginnings until very recently, swags, wreaths and garlands were always composed on circlets or ropes made from long, supple stems. Country folk and children wove wreath bases from dry but pliable grasses, bryony, sheep's parsley and other suitable stems, and decorated them with colourful wild flowers or sungold grains and seedheads. Today, however, a wide variety of wreath bases are available, ranging from chunky ones made of willow stems or tightly intertwined vine stems, to moss-covered wire wreath forms and practical pre-formed rings of dry or absorbent floral foam.

Wreaths, swags and garlands incorporating plant material are basically flower arrangements without a visible container, and are among the oldest forms of floral decoration. Whether composed from evergreen foliage decorated with bright seasonal fruits, or from delicately coloured early-spring flowers, they can brighten our homes throughout the year.

Whereas flowers are the decorations most associated with swags, wreaths and garlands, some stunning effects are possible using fabrics (or even crepe paper or foil) as a basis for decoration. Not only do they offer infinite scope in the choice of materials, but they can incorporate a variety of traditional needlecrafts, including patchwork and appliqué. Yet it is equally easy to create lovely designs with little or no needlework experience.

All of the projects in this book are suitable for novices but will appeal to experienced flower arrangers and needleworkers as well. Basic techniques are explained in the Techniques section at the end of the book, and techniques that are more specific to a project are covered in the instructions for that design.

Most of the equipment you will already have, so these tools are not included under the materials for each project, but any specialist equipment is listed, together with all materials. For the floral projects you will need floral foam — either absorbent foam, which is for fresh plant materials and is soaked in water for a few minutes before use, or dry foam, which is for dry plant materials and cannot be soaked. Both types come in blocks or rounds and can be cut to size. You'll also need fine silver floral wire, which comes in a reel (spool), and medium-gauge stub wires. Wire cutters are essential for cutting stub wires. For fabric-based projects, you will need a large pair of scissors for cutting out fabric, a small, pointed pair for sewing, and possibly a pair of pinking shears; a tape measure, needles and pins; and possibly a sewing machine. PVA glue (white glue in the U.S.) and a good craft knife are useful for both types of project.

The most important ingredient, however, is inspiration, and that is what this book aims to provide. Try a few of the projects — you'll soon find it hard to stop creating these attractive showpieces.

DESIGN IDEAS

*With their wonderful colours and
graceful shapes, swags, wreaths and garlands
add style to any setting and any occasion.*

Whether it is a circlet of fresh flowers worn by a young bridesmaid, a Christmas wreath hanging on the front door to welcome visitors, a leafy garland draped around a party table or a graceful swag of muslin bound with ribbons and flowers — a swag, wreath or garland makes an enchanting decoration.

If you use fresh flowers, these will, of course, be dependent upon the time of year, so let your arrangement be a celebration of the changing seasons. In spring, for instance, you could combine ivy with violets and primroses, or with narcissus and grape hyacinth. In summer, try nasturtiums with feverfew, roses with gypsophila (baby's breath), or alstroemeria with alchemilla (lady's mantle). In autumn, combine rosehips with vivid autumn leaves, and in winter berried holly with skimmia.

Don't underestimate the value of leaves. Offering an enormous variety of colours, shapes and textures, they are ideal both as a background to flowers and as interesting elements of the design.

Many people turn to dried flowers only in winter, but there is such a wonderful range of subtle colours and varied textures available today that they deserve to be enjoyed all year round. They can be used with any of a vast range of different materials, including dried grasses, grains, seedheads, preserved leaves, dried apple and orange rings, dried mushrooms, nuts, cones, spices (such as cinnamon sticks, nutmegs, star anise, chilli peppers), dried herbs, moss, lichen, twigs, feathers, shells and driftwood.

Don't be afraid to combine dried materials with fresh; flowers with fruit; common wild flowers like cow parsley or Queen Anne's lace with florist's flowers; houseplant foliage with cut flowers; pussy willow or catkins with spring flowers.

Similarly, be open-minded about how you treat the

*Left: In this splendid harvest swag, gourds and thistles, seedheads
and quails' eggs offer a wealth of contrasting sizes and shapes,
textures and colours. The dramatic tassels add to the feeling of
richness and abundance.*

Opposite: Brambles twisted into a wreath shape form a natural base for clusters of autumnal glycerined leaves and ferns, glistening rose hips, moss, leucodendron and dyed broom bloom.

Right: Dried sweetcorn, barley, Chinese lanterns and red apples are composed into a group of harmonizing decorations for Thanksgiving or harvest festival.

Below: Dried roses, larkspur and love-in-a-mist seedheads create a romantic bridal headdress and posy.

plant material. For example, gilding or touching lightly with gold paint (or white paint for a frosted effect) can be effective, particularly at Christmas. Some flower arrangers, inspired by the splendid limewood swags of the 17th century British woodcarver Grinling Gibbons, make dried flower swags which they paint gold over matt black. Nuts, seedheads, small gourds and cones are included, as well as ribbons, scallop shells, cherubs, miniature musical instruments and other decorative shapes. A lighter version of this sort of swag can be painted white in imitation of the 18th century plasterwork swags by Robert Adam.

At the other end of the spectrum are the charming wreaths based on a relatively simple idea. For example, try winding supple twigs around a coat hanger bent into a heart shape, and then wiring bunches of berries and pine cones to the twigs. Or make a garland by threading onto wire dried eucalyptus leaves and apple or orange slices, or dried bay leaves, dried chillies and cinnamon sticks, then tying the ends of the garland with torn strips of checked fabric.

The more swags, wreaths or garlands you make, the more skilled you will become at composing attractive arrangements. There are no hard-and-fast rules about design, but the following guidelines may help.

The colours you use are what make the greatest impression. If the swag, wreath or garland is for a dark corner, use colours like white, cream, yellow, orange or pale tints of other hues. Very effective colour schemes can be devised using just one colour in its tints (the pure hue with white added — also called pastels), tones (with grey added) shades (with black added), or using colours close to each other in the spectrum, such as cream, yellow, apricot, orange and brown.

Contrasting colours, especially vibrant primary colours, can look dramatic but are harder to handle. Sometimes, though, it helps to use tints and shades rather than the pure hues — for example, pink, cream and navy rather than red, yellow and blue. This sort of

Above: Focus all eyes on a wedding or christening cake with a sheer muslin swag bound with contrasting ribbons and pearl trim and decorated with flower posies.

Left: This exuberant table swag includes globe artichokes and protea buds among the tightly clustered dried summer flowers and seedheads. The materials range in size from the fluffy "pompons" and heads of the artichokes through peonies and hydrangeas to love-in-a-mist and poppy heads.

colour scheme is usually more pleasing if one colour predominates, especially when any complementary colours (red/green, yellow/purple, orange/blue) are being used together.

In an arrangement using lots of colours, it's important to maintain an overall balance. This does not mean dotting the colours about, which just creates a monotonous blur. Instead, try to group the colours.

A successful arrangement makes good use of both variation and repetition in colour, texture and shape. Try to use some matt and some glossy materials, since a predominantly matt texture will look flat and uninteresting, while too many glossy surfaces will just cancel each other out. Similarly, try to include a variety of shapes and sizes (avoiding extremes of large and small, which would look out of proportion).

Because wreaths, garlands and swags have their outlines already established, you can start by arranging the larger, more rounded shapes, which will be the focal points. In a horizontal swag, the vertical drops will include more of the longer, thinner material, though you should try to keep the main forms, colours and textures roughly the same in the drops as on the rest of the swag. Now fill in with the bushy plant and background material.

Make some of the clusters substantial enough to add fullness and visual weight, bearing in mind that three of something is more interesting than two or four. Make use of curving stems to emphasize curves, and try to make the overall shape bold and well-defined.

Experiment with placement of the plant materials before you wire them on, and stand back and check the effect frequently as you work. Ultimately, what *you* think looks right is all that matters.

Once hung, a horizontal swag should look balanced — the curves should be of equal thickness and the two vertical drops the same length. A vertical swag can be wide at the top and tapering to a point, or it can be "waisted", with sections of varying widths.

It is generally a good idea to err on the side of understatement and simplicity — no one wants to be accused of gilding the lily — but sometimes beautiful big bows will finish off wreaths, garlands or swags to perfection. Whether wire-edged or organdie, moiré taffeta or tartan, the ribbons available today are spectacular; you may even be inspired to use a ribbon as your starting point. Paper ribbon, with its subtle colours and matt texture, harmonizes especially well with the soft tones of dried flowers.

Fabrics too are well suited to the wreath and swag shapes and can be used with or without flowers. Decorated with ribbon or lace, with braids, beads or buttons, with silk flowers or sequins, fabric wreaths, swags and garlands can look sensational. On a swag made of heavy fabric, cording or fringe can follow the sweep of the swag, while lighter fabric looks good with a lightweight bobble fringe or garland of silk flowers. First decide on a theme, then sort out all the trinkets and trims that sum up that idea. Design it around an occasion, or create something that will look fabulous all year round.

Left: The elegant curves of the gilded mirror are repeated in the shallow drapes of the evergreen and flower garland decorating this mantelpiece. The gilding is echoed by clusters of gold-sprayed dried hydrangeas and poppy seedheads, which contrast strongly in both form and style with fan-shaped bunches of waxy white lilies near the ends. A crimson ribbon and tiny Christmas tree lights running through the evergreen foliage add a seasonal note.

Opposite: Composed in traditional red and green, a splendid evergreen wreath draws attention to a doorway that itself holds out a warm welcome to visitors at Christmas. The tub of brilliant scarlet poinsettias reinforces the depth of the colour highlights in the other decorative details.

15

FRESH PLANT MATERIAL

From leafy swags and wreaths embellished with glossy fruits and spices, to dainty bridal headdresses and party-table garlands, the designs in this chapter draw on a wide variety of fresh materials to give an exciting new look to traditional decorations for everyday and special occasions.

Bridal headdress • Springtime celebration ring
Wedding table ring • Pine garland
Christmas wreath • Apple and spice wreath
Vegetable ring • Table garland • Ribbon swag

BRIDAL HEADDRESS

*A pretty circlet of flowers worn as a headdress by a young bride or bridesmaid is
one of the most enchanting examples of a floral garland. Match the flowers to those in the
bride's bouquet and to the table flowers for a totally coordinated look.*

MATERIALS
length of pliable, plastic-coated wire
fine silver floral wire
*satin ribbon in a colour to tone with
    the flowers*
*selection of flowers such as small
    roses, spray chrysanthemums and
    Peruvian lilies (alstroemeria)*
*pale, long-lasting leaves such as
    variegated ivy or scented geranium*

1 Measure the plastic-coated wire so
that it will form a hoop that fits
comfortably on the head. Using wire
cutters, cut the wire to allow for an
overlap. Cross over the two ends and
bind them securely with fine silver
floral wire.

2 Bind the wire ring with the ribbon,
overlapping the ribbon all the way
around until the wire is completely
covered. Tie and fasten off the ribbon.

3 Cut the flower stems to a length of
about 4 in (10 cm) and separate
them into groups of each type. Take one

or two stems from each group, along
with two or three leaves, and arrange
them to make small posies. Bind the
stems with fine floral wire *(bottom of
previous column)*.

4 Put the posies in cool water in a
cool, dark place until you are ready
to assemble the headdress.

5 Using fine floral wire, bind the first
posy onto the ring, with the
flowerheads lying flat against it.

6 Place the second posy so that the
flowerheads cover the stems of the
one before, and bind it in place *(below)*.
Continue binding on the posies until
the ring is complete.

7 Tie a small ribbon bow and leave
long, trailing ends. Cut the ends
slantwise to neaten them.

8 Thread a short length of wire
through the back of the loop, and
bind the bow to the headdress *(top of
next column)*.

VARIATIONS
• For a summery variation, blend
lady's mantle *(Alchemilla mollis)* with
ranunculus, spray carnations and roses.
• There is no need to avoid flowers
formed on long spires or in thick
clusters. If the bride's favourite flowers
are blue delphiniums or cream orchids,
for example, cut each flower from the
main stem and bind the stemlets with
fine floral wire. Conceal the wire among
the bunched stems of the posies.

HINTS
When you have completed the
headdress, spray it lightly with
cool water and keep it in a cool,
dark place. A low shelf of the
refrigerator is ideal.
    If you have to take the
headdress some distance, pack it
in crumpled tissue paper in a box
that just fits it, such as an old
hatbox. Take a few spare flowers
with you in case any are
damaged on the journey. Wrap
the stems in wet tissues, place the
flowers in a plastic bag and seal it
with a twist-tie.

SPRINGTIME CELEBRATION RING

Celebrate the coming of spring or a special family occasion with a lovely table centrepiece composed of the season's prettiest flowers. The cluster of tapers offsets the symmetricality of the ring shape, adding another dimension to the arrangement.

MATERIALS
pre-formed absorbent foam ring, 10in (25cm) in diameter
selection of fresh flowers such as narcissus "Cheerfulness", grape hyacinth (muscari), mimosa, heather and hellebores
short sprays of foliage or separate leaves such as variegated ivy or scented geranium
tapers

1 As soon as you bring the flowers indoors, recut all the stem ends at a sharp angle, to enable them to take up water more easily. Put the flowers in a bucket of tepid water and leave them in a cool, dark place for several hours, or preferably overnight.

2 Soak the ring in water for up to an hour, until the foam is well saturated. When you start to assemble the wreath, remember to work on a stain-resistant surface that will not be damaged by moisture.

3 Position the tapers in a cluster at one side of the ring *(below)*. If you wish to add visual interest, cut short lengths from some of the tapers to stagger the heights.

4 Sort through the foliage you have selected, and cut the stems to short, even lengths of about 1in (2.5cm). In this way, the leaves will be positioned close against the foam and will go a long way towards concealing it.

5 Arrange the foliage around the inner and outer rims of the ring, with the leaves or sprays facing in a variety of directions. Position some leaves almost vertically around the sides of the ring, so that they cover the plastic base. You might find it more convenient to complete small sections of the ring at a time *(below)*.

6 Arrange short stems of a "filler" flower such as heather among the foliage all around the ring. This will create the impression of a carpet of flowers on which more vibrant blooms will be arranged.

7 Arrange a cluster of tall, slender flowers, such as grape hyacinths and mimosa, around the tapers so that they appear to be growing among them *(top of next column)*.

8 Cut short stems of hellebores so that the flowers form clusters of three or four. If you do this in advance of composing the ring, keep the stems in a shallow dish of water.

9 Position clusters of hellebores at intervals around the ring *(below)*, close together, and with some trailing over the rim. *(Continued on page 23)*

10 Cut short stems of narcissus and keep these, too, in water until just before you arrange them. Position them in clusters among the hellebores, with some flowers trailing low over the inner and outer rims *(below)*.

11 Arrange groups of two or three grape hyacinths among other flowers, to contrast their deep blue colour with the paler shades.

12 Turn the ring around and look at it closely from every angle, to check whether there are any gaps. If there are, fill them in with foliage sprays and heather.

Opposite: To create this spectacular wedding table ring, use the same basic approach as for the springtime celebration ring, but replace the cluster of tapers with four dinner candles. For details see Variation.

VARIATION

• This design makes a beautiful **wedding table ring** (see photograph opposite), especially when decorated with four dinner candles instead of tapers. Arrange them at equal intervals around the circle, in the style of an Advent ring. The candles should be in colours that tone perfectly with one of the flower types, or that are in sharp contrast (here, miniature white tulips, spray carnations, white freesias, baby's breath, pulmonia, and willow leaves). Deep blue candles, for example, would be a perfect match for the grape hyacinths in the floral ring shown on page 21. Insert each candle in a plastic candle spike *(below)*, which is available from florists, to avoid breaking up the soaked foam.

HINTS

Tapers have a relatively short burning time, which will be shortened still further if you cut them to uneven lengths. Keep a spare bundle of tapers handy so that, as they burn down, you can insert new ones, lighting them from the original ones.

Do not allow tapers or candles to burn so low that the flames are near the flowers or foliage.

Never leave lighted tapers or candles unattended in a room. Leaving them for even a short while is a fire hazard.

To keep the flowers fresh for as long as possible, remove the ring to a moisture-proof surface and spray it with cool water every day. Avoid spraying tulips and daffodils, however, or the leaves will turn papery.

23

PINE GARLAND

In the spirit of Christmas past, decorate a fireplace, door or window with a fragrant garland of pine branches hung with colourful dried orange rings. It looks spectacular yet is not difficult to make.

MATERIALS
articulated core of soaked foam blocks
blue pine branches
evergreens, such as juniper and ivy
dried orange rings (see page 29)
Chinese star anise seedpods
hot glue, or clear all-purpose glue
medium-gauge stub wires
pine cones
3in (7.5cm)-wide ribbon

The type of garland core shown in the photographs can be bought at some florists' or by mail order (see Sources of Supply). It consists of small plastic "cages" which are filled with absorbent floral foam and then hooked together to form a continuous, articulated chain. Alternatively, you can make your own garland core by wrapping soaked blocks of absorbent floral foam in chickenwire for a few minutes and then wiring them together. There are full instructions for making an absorbent-foam garland core in the Techniques section.

1 Measure the area to be decorated by the garland, allowing extra length for any drapes you wish it to have, then make or link together a core of the appropriate length. If the garland is to be hung against a surface that will be damaged by moisture, wrap the soaked foam blocks in clingfilm (plastic wrap) before enclosing them in the plastic "cage" or the chicken wire.

2 Cut short lengths of blue pine and any other evergreens, and insert them into the foam blocks *(top of next column)* until the core is completely covered by the foliage.

3 Using either clear all-purpose glue, or a glue gun (see page 32), stick a star anise seedpod to the centre of each dried orange ring *(below)*.

4 Cut stub wires in half with wire cutters and push each through a ring. Twist the ends together close to the rim.

5 Attach the orange rings to the garland by pushing the wires between the evergreens and into the foam *(top of next column)*. Check that no wires are visible. Wire pine cones as described on page 29, and push the wires into the garland.

6 Tie the ribbon into full bows and neaten the ends. Thread a stub wire through the back of each loop.

7 If you wish to hang the garland on the wall, make a hanging loop at the back of the garland near each end, as shown in the Techniques section. You may also wish to add one or more hanging loops in between these two, the number depending on the actual length of the garland you've made.

8 Hang the garland in position, or, if preferred, lay it along the top of a mantelpiece or picture frame.

9 Attach the bows in the centre or at each "peak" by pushing the stub wires into the foam.

HINTS
If you display the garland on the mantelpiece, remember never to allow it to hang near the fire. Be sure always to use a firescreen on the fire.

To protect the mantelpiece, you could back the wired areas with parcel tape or green felt.

CHRISTMAS WREATH

Make a wreath of mixed evergreens chosen for their contrasting textures and colours, and then decorate it with small, glossy fruits. The rich tones and rough surfaces of the greenery provide the perfect foil for the bright, shiny fruits.

1 Cover the wire ring frame with moss, as shown in the Techniques section. There is no need to fasten off the binding twine at the end; you can leave it to start binding on the evergreen foliage.

2 Sort through the evergreens. Snip off any damaged or discoloured leaves, and any bare side stems. If large glossy leaves such as ivy look a little dusty, rub them with a clean, dry cloth.

3 Cut the evergreen stems to roughly equal lengths, about 6in (15cm), and gather them into mixed bunches of three or four stems. Bind the stems with fine floral wire, to make it easier to secure the bunches to the ring *(below)*.

4 Place the first bunch over the covered ring frame and bind it in place, taking the twine over and around the frame several times.

5 Position the second bunch of evergreens on the ring so that the tips of the leaves cover the stem ends of the first bunch. Bind the bunch to the frame as before *(below)*.

6 Continue binding on bunches of evergreens until the ring is covered all around, then tie and cut off the end of the twine.

7 Thread the kumquats onto the pliable wire *(below)* so that they form a continuous ring to fit around the inside of the evergreen wreath.

8 Check that the kumquat ring fits neatly inside the wreath, then twist the two free ends of the wire together *(below)*, leaving them ready to attach to the wreath.

9 Hold the fruit ring in place inside the wreath. Push the free wire ends through the wreath and bend them over to secure the fruit ring in place.

10 Fasten the fruit ring and wreath together at the opposite end by twisting a stub wire around them both.

11 If you will want to hang the Christmas wreath on the wall or a door, from a hanging loop, make a hanging loop using a medium-gauge stub wire as shown in the Techniques section.

VARIATIONS
• Small fruits nestling among the leaves give the evergreen wreath a completely different look. Kumquats, satsumas, limes, small pomegranates, lychees and apples are all suitable. Raffia-tied bundles of cinnamon sticks also look good, especially when combined with apples in an **apple and spice wreath** (see photograph on page 28). (*Continued on page 29*)

To wire apples or other fruits to the wreath, thread a medium-gauge stub wire through each one close to the base then twist the two ends of the wire together beneath the fruit *(above)*.

To wire a cinnamon-stick bundle, push a stub wire through the raffia at the back and twist the ends together.

Fix the fruits and cinnamon-stick bundle to the wreath by pushing the wires through the evergreens to the

Opposite: Instead of the inner ring of kumquats used in the Christmas wreath, experiment with random arrangements of colourful fruits and cinnamon-stick bundles wired to the wreath, as in this apple and spice ring. *For details see Variations.*

back of the ring and bending them outwards *(below)*.

• As an alternative decoration, and one entirely in keeping with the evergreens, you could decorate the wreath with pine cones instead of with the fruit ring. To do this, wrap a stub wire around each cone, close to the base. Bring the two ends of the wire together and twist them. Push the wires into the wreath at intervals, bending them over to secure.

• Dried apple rings look wonderful in a wreath of this sort. Slice uncored deep red or bright green apples crosswise to a thickness of about $1/8$in (3mm). Place them immediately in a brine of 2 tablespoons salt to 3 imperial pints/$7^{1/2}$ cups (1.8 litres) water. Leave for 10 minutes then pat dry with paper towels. Thread the rings onto string and hang them in a warm place for several days until they are leathery.

• The orange rings used in the garland on pages 24-5 look equally effective in an evergreen wreath like this. You may be able to buy dried orange rings in florists' or gift shops, but they are easy to make yourself. Preheat the oven to the lowest setting, cut the fruits into $1/4$in (6mm) slices and pat them dry with paper towels. Place the slices in single layers on wire racks and dry them in the oven for six to eight hours, until they are tough and leathery. Turn the orange rings once during this time.

• For a completely different look, and a pleasantly pungent aroma, you could use the same basic techniques to make a wreath of evergreen herbs. Arrange the herbs when they are fresh, then leave them to dry gradually on the wreath in a warm, airy room. Attractive and long-lasting herbs that would be suitable include bay, rosemary, sage, purple sage, lavender, artemisia and thyme. They could be grouped into small bunches of

separate types, or mixed for a more random look. Once you have covered the ring with herb foliage, you can decorate it further with flowering herbs, such as marjoram, oregano, tansy, lavender, santolina and thyme, which will also dry well in situ. If you plan to have the wreath in the kitchen, you could add small "dolly-bags" of spice seeds or pot-pourri tied into pouches made of muslin or cotton gingham.

HINTS

Part of the appeal of the wreath with the kumquat ring is its symmetry. With wreaths such as the apple and spice version, however, it is better to aim for balance rather than actual symmetry. Also, remember that the wreath will be seen from the front (and, to a lesser extent, from the sides) so it will need to be covered evenly.

To keep evergreen wreaths looking fresh, spray with water every day. Conditioning the branches by standing them in water for a few hours before assembling the wreath will also help it to last longer.

VEGETABLE RING

Bundles of young vegetables, as varied as possible, make an unusual and attractive table centre. The vine wreath and the raffia ties add to the natural, wholesome effect of the arrangement. This centrepiece is sure to become a talking point!

MATERIALS
vine wreath base, 10in (25cm) in diameter
selection of young, small vegetables such as green beans, mange-touts (snow peas), baby sweetcorn, spring onions (scallions) and carrots
raffia
medium-gauge stub wires
fresh herbs

1 Grade each vegetable type according to size, sorting them out into long, medium and shorter lengths.

2 Gather the vegetables into small bundles, about 2in (5cm) in diameter. Tie each one with several strands of raffia *(below)* and trim off the raffia ends.

3 Cut the stub wires in half with wire cutters. Push a length of wire through the raffia at the back of each vegetable bundle, taking care not to pierce the vegetables with the wire.

4 Attach the first vegetable bundle to the vine wreath base, pushing the wires between the woody stems in order to secure them.

5 Place the vegetable bundles in an order which shows each type to best advantage, contrasting neighbouring ones for colour, shape and texture *(below)*.

6 Wire on more vegetable bundles at varying angles *(below)* until covered all the way around. Check as you work that it looks balanced.

7 Keep the herb sprays in water until just before the meal, then tuck them among the vegetables to give the wreath a light and refreshing aroma.

VARIATIONS
• Cover only about three-quarters of the vine wreath base with vegetable bundles, then make a bow from paper ribbon or from many strands of raffia and fix it to the ring with a stub wire in the remaining quarter of the wreath, where you have not placed any of the vegetable bundles.
• To add some flashes of brighter colour, you could dot a few chilli peppers around the wreath among the more softly toned vegetables.

HINT
If you keep the vegetables or the completed wreath in the refrigerator until just before putting it on display, and return them when the occasion is over, the food will not be wasted, as you will be able to cook and serve the vegetables the next day.

TABLE GARLAND

When a party table is all set to become the centre of attention, encircle it with a garland of fresh flower posies bound to paper ribbon and decorated with paper-ribbon bows, in a colour scheme to match the occasion.

MATERIALS
tightly furled paper ribbon
fine silver floral wire
trails of foliage such as ruscus or sprengrii, from florists
selection of fresh flowers such as freesias, spray chrysanthemums and gypsophila (baby's breath)
medium-gauge stub wires

1 For a small table, measure around the rim. For a long buffet table, measure across the front fall of the tablecloth, allowing for any drapes you wish the garland to have. Cut the paper ribbon to the required length for the core, allowing extra for an overlap.

2 Using fine floral wire, bind long trails of foliage to the paper-ribbon core, without unfurling the paper ribbon, and making sure that the tips of each bunch cover the stems of the one before *(below)*.

3 Cut the flower stems to roughly equal lengths, about 3in (7.5cm). Separate the flowers according to type,

then gather them into a variety of mixed bunches, to give the garland an informal look.

4 Bind the posy stems with fine floral wire, and stand them in a shallow dish of water until you are ready to assemble the garland.

5 Cut stub wires in half with wire cutters, bend into U-shapes and use these to attach the posies to the garland, concealing the stems among the foliage sprays *(below)*. If the posies twist, it may be necessary to attach them at both the stem and tip ends.

6 If you wish to decorate the garland with paper-ribbon bows, unfurl the paper ribbon and cut it into equal

lengths. Slightly scrunch it up again, then twist each length into the shape of a letter "M". Cross the two loops of the "M" over each other *(bottom of previous column)*, tie them into a knot and pull it tightly. Ease out the knot to neaten it, then ease out the loops until they are full and rounded.

7 Wire any bows onto the garland once it is in place, and cut the ends slantwise to neaten them.

VARIATIONS
• If you wish to give the garland a subtle and pleasing aroma, you could use variegated apple mint in place of the more formal foliage.
• If the party is to be held outdoors, and there is any likelihood of rain, it is best not to use paper ribbon for the garland core and bows. Choose an unobtrusive green wire or natural, twisted cord for the core, and cotton or synthetic silk ribbon.

HINTS
If you prefer, you can glue the posies instead of wiring them to the foliage garland. Use a hot-glue gun if you have one, or clear all-purpose glue. Run a little of the glue along the stems, press them onto the paper-ribbon core and hold them in place for a few seconds.

If you use hot glue, take special care not to get any on your fingers, because it can burn. Once a hot-glue gun is plugged in, never leave it unattended, and take extra care when using the appliance if there are young children nearby.

RIBBON SWAG

Hidden underneath this slender vertical swag, with its generous paper-ribbon
bow and long trails, is soaked floral foam, which keeps the flowers fresh for as long as possible.
A pair of these could be displayed on either side of a fireplace, door or window.

The foam core is made by wrapping the soaked foam blocks in clingfilm (plastic wrap), then placing them in purchased plastic "cages" which hook together (see Source of Supply). Use only the bottom half of the cages, securing the foam in place with floral tape. Alternatively, you could make your own version as described in the Techniques section.

1 Tie a paper ribbon bow and attach it to the top of the foam core with a bent stub wire *(below)*.

2 Cut two lengths of the paper ribbon. Cut stub wires in half with wire cutters, and twist one around one end of each length of ribbon. Push both into the lower end of the base.

3 Cut short sprays of viburnum. Use a fine skewer to make holes in the clingfilm and arrange the sprays to partly cover the base.

4 Arrange long sprays of foliage to trail from the lower end of the decoration and short sprays to rise almost vertically from the foam, angling the sprays to give the design dimension and height *(below)*.

5 Cut the Peruvian lilies on short stems and arrange them throughout the decoration *(below)*. Cut off any of the leaves which look too straggly.

6 Fill in the decoration with short stems of spray chrysanthemums, using some of the buds for variation.

7 If desired, make a hanging loop for the swag, as described in the Techniques section.

8 Spray the decoration with cool water, taking care to avoid soaking the paper ribbon.

DRIED FLOWERS AND SEEDHEADS

The designs in this section draw on a wide variety of long-lasting natural materials, ranging from sweet-scented herbs and romantic flowers to exotic seedheads and glistening shells. With soft colours, lingering fragrance and intricate textures, these are the raw materials of some memorable decorations.

Seashore wreath • Exotic seedhead wreath
Country wreath • Scented swag
Romantic table ring • Dried-flower heart

SEASHORE WREATH

A walk on the beach, a basket of holiday mementoes, or a treasure-hunting trip to speciality and craft shops will yield a medley of wave-lashed and sun-bleached materials you can compose into a seashore wreath.

1 Sort out the various categories of materials you have gathered and arrange them in a circle, to see how they shape up in terms of colour balance and texture. Move them around until you find the arrangement pleasing.

2 Cut the sea lavender and other flower stems into short lengths and form them into bunches of a single colour or mixed shades. Bind the stems with fine floral wire.

3 Cut some of the stub wires in half with wire cutters and bend them into U-shapes. Attach each flower bunch to the wreath base with one of these *(bottom of previous column)*.

4 Attach large thistles or globe artichoke heads and pieces of coral in a similar way, with more U-shaped wires.

5 Using clear glue or a glue gun, attach groups of shells at intervals around the wreath and on the coral, overlapping and overlaying them to give a clustered effect *(below)*.

6 Glue clusters of dried seaweed in place on the wreath, positioning them so that they contrast in colour and in texture with the shells.

7 Fill in any gaps in the design by gluing on clumps of lichen or of reindeer moss, and tuck in a few feathers at random angles.

8 Tie a fairly large bow in the length of cord or rope, and attach it to the wreath with a bent stub wire *(top of next column)*.

VARIATIONS
• For a greater variety of texture and colour you could include stems of bright yellow, purple and magenta dried statice, which is readily available in florists' shops.
• To give the wreath an even more authentic "beachcombing" pedigree, you could also include small pieces of bleached driftwood or oddly shaped twigs.

EXOTIC SEEDHEAD WREATH

*Incorporating a collection of exotic-looking dried seedheads and stems in tones
ranging from sun-bleached cream to woody brown, this lovely wreath has strong textural
interest and an almost architectural quality.*

MATERIALS
*vine wreath base, 10in (25cm) in
diameter
selection of dried stems and
seedheads such as lotus heads,
protea, plumosum, golden
mushrooms, miniature sweetcorn,
dryandra, bottlebrush, Madeira
flowers and larch cones,
medium-gauge stub wires
hot glue, or clear all-purpose glue*

1 Sort through the dried plant
materials and arrange and re-
arrange them in a circular shape until
you achieve a balance you find
pleasing. Check that none of the items
is too large or heavy-looking for the
scale of the decoration.

2 Look carefully at the main
seedheads and other decorative
materials and assess which ones can
easily be mounted on wires, and which
can more easily be glued in position.

3 Gather into bunches short lengths
of dried stems such as dryandra
and bottlebrush, and bind them with

stub wires. Position at intervals around
the ring. Push the wires between the
gaps *(bottom of previous column)* and
twist them at the back.

4 Wire suitable materials such as
lotus heads, which have a soft
texture, and golden mushrooms, which
have a sharply pointed conical shape.
Twist the wire ends together beneath
the plant material *(below)*.

5 Glue into place a central feature
such as a multi-segmented
"buddha" seedpod *(below)*, then glue
other materials such as dried sweetcorn
cobs and larch cones so that they
appear to radiate from it.

6 Build up the design by working
outwards in each direction from
the central feature, contrasting shapes
and colours as much as possible.

7 Glue on small materials such as
"bell cup" seedpods and pubescens
heads to cover wires and bunched
stems, or to draw attention to large
items such as conical-shaped
mushrooms.

HINTS
Variation is inevitable in a design
that uses a selection of widely
different plant materials, leaving
you plenty of scope for
imaginative inter-pretations of
the decoration.
　Try to use a combination of
slender stems and rounded
shapes, and both matt and glossy
textures. Do not feel that you
have to cover the whole of the
wreath base. The rugged twigs
blend well with the woody
decorative materials.
　Look out for boxes or bags of
"exotic" seedheads in florists'
shops. Some sell ready-made
selections of these mainly
Amazonian dried plants, which
would be ideal to compose into a
wreath of this kind.

COUNTRY WREATH

Here, pretty country-garden flowers and scented flowering herbs decorate a ring covered with paper ribbon. Colourful and unsophisticated, it would make a charming wallhanging in a young girl's bedroom.

MATERIALS
double copper wire ring frame (from florists), 10in (25cm) in diameter
paper ribbon
selection of dried flowers such as strawflowers, roses, dyed sea lavender and marjoram
fine silver floral wire
hot glue, or clear all-purpose glue
1 stub wire (optional)

1 Unfurl a length of paper ribbon and use it to wrap around the wire ring frame, as explained in the Techniques section.

2 Cut the stems of the dried flowers to a length of about 4in (10cm) from tip to stem end.

3 Compose small bunches of mixed materials and colours, including one or two strawflowers and a rose in each bunch. Bind the stems with silver wire *(below)*.

4 Run a line of glue along the stems on the reverse of one bunch and press it onto the paper-ribbon-covered ring. If you are using hot glue, take care not to get any on your fingers, and keep it away from children.

5 Continue around the ring, gluing on each bunch so that the tips of the flowers cover the stem ends of the one before *(below)*. Leave an area at the top of the ring which is undecorated with flowers.

6 Unfurl a length of the paper ribbon, partly scrunch it up again and form it into the shape of an "M". Cross over the two loops and tie a knot. Ease out the loops and cut the ends slantwise to neaten them.

7 Stick the bow onto the ring and decorate the loop with a few flowers or a small posy *(bottom of previous column)*.

8 If desired, make a hanging loop from a stub wire, as directed in the Techniques section.

VARIATIONS
• A wreath of this kind lends itself to a variety of colour schemes. For a cool, fresh look choose pale green hydrangea, yellow roses and undyed sea lavender. For a more vibrant effect, you could use orange-dyed sea lavender, bright orange and yellow strawflowers and red roses.

SCENTED SWAG

The mingled aromas of cinnamon sticks and flowers gathered and dried at the height of summer add a charming dimension to a vertical swag. Based on a straw plait, it makes a delightful wall or table decoration.

MATERIALS
*thick straw plait, 24in (60cm) long,
    from florists
long cinnamon sticks
selection of dried flowers such as
    larkspur, strawflowers, carthamus,
    roses and hydrangea
selection of dried seedheads such as
    poppy, love-in-a-mist, Chinese
    lanterns (physalis or winter
    cherry) and linseed (flax)
fine silver floral wire
raffia
1 or 2 medium-gauge stub wires*

1 Divide the dried flowers and other plant materials into two roughly equal groups to help you to create a balanced design.

2 Take three or four cinnamon sticks and arrange a few long-stemmed flowers and seedheads among them *(below)*, with the tips of some of the flowers extending beyond the cinnamon sticks.

3 Bind the stems and the cinnamon sticks with fine floral wire to hold them firmly in place, then position over one end of the plait.

4 Add more materials to the bunch, choosing those with progressively shorter stems so that the flowers and seedheads are at graduated heights. Bind the stems with fine floral wire, then cover the wire with raffia *(below)*.

5 Make a similar though not necessarily identical bunch with the second group of dried materials.

6 Place the two bundles end to end on the straw plait, with the stem ends of each one meeting in the centre. Bind the bunches securely to the plait with raffia.

7 Pull out a handful of raffia strands from a skein and bind them around the centre of the plait, to conceal where the two bunches meet. Tie more raffia in a large, straggly bow and attach it to the centre of the plait with the stub wire *(top of next column)*.

8 If desired, make a hanging loop on the back at the top of the swag with a stub wire, as directed in the Techniques section.

VARIATIONS
• To give the swag a harvest-time look, you could include long straws of wheat, oats or barley among the dried flowers.
• At Christmas you could add clusters of cones close to the centre and decorate the swag with a coloured ribbon bow in place of the raffia.

ROMANTIC TABLE RING

Lavender and roses, hydrangeas and peonies, strawflowers and lady's mantle —
the evocative, old-fashioned flowers in this sweet-smelling table ring keep alive the colours
and scents of a country garden in summer.

MATERIALS
dried stem ring, 10in (25cm) in
   diameter
selection of dried flowers such as
   lavender, roses, hydrangea, peonies,
   strawflowers and lady's mantle
   (Alchemilla mollis)
glycerine-preserved leaves, such as
   eucalyptus
medium-gauge stub wires
fine silver floral wire
clear all-purpose glue
sheer ribbon, 2in (5cm) wide

1 If some of the flowers have been dried in a desiccant such as silica gel crystals and have short stems, or none at all, you may decide to mount them on false stems made of wire.

2 Use stub wires to mount peonies that have been dried without stems (and are therefore less expensive to buy). Push a wire up through the centre of a flower from below. Bend it into a small hook at the top *(below)* and pull the wire down so that the hook is concealed within the flower.

3 To wire flowers such as roses that have been dried on short stems, place a stub wire parallel to the stem

(below). Use fine floral wire to bind them together, then cut the false wire stem to the length you require.

4 Gather the lavender into small bunches, cut the stems to a total length of about 4in (10cm) and bind them together with fine floral wire.

5 Make several posies of four or five rosebuds, and bind the stems together with fine floral wire. Take care not to crush or crowd the flowers.

6 Cut short sprays of eucalyptus leaves and of lady's mantle. Take two or three stems of each type and bind them into bunches with fine floral wire. Cut the hydrangeas into small clusters of florets.

7 Cut several stub wires in half with wire cutters, and bend them into U-shapes. Begin to assemble the wreath by arranging the hydrangea clusters and the eucalyptus and lady's mantle bunches around it. Fix them in place by pushing the bent wires over the stems and into the wreath base *(top of next column).*

8 If the peonies are mounted on wires, bend the wire stems slightly sideways and push them firmly into the stem ring. If they have natural stems, attach them with stub wires. Glue a stemless rose in the centre of each peony *(below).*

9 In a similar way attach the bunches of rosebuds and lavender that have been found together *(top of first column, page 49).* Position them at varying angles so that the completed wreath will look good from all viewpoints. *(Continued on page 49)*

10 Fill in any gaps in the design with sprays of eucalyptus and lady's mantle and with clusters of strawflowers. Turn the ring around and check that it looks good from all angles. Snip off any damaged or broken leaves, and any broken or bare stems.

11 Tie the ribbon into a bow, cut the ends slantwise and fasten it onto the ring with a U-shaped wire.

VARIATIONS

• A moss-covered ring bent into the shape of a heart makes an attractive alternative to a stem ring base. The **dried-flower heart** in the photograph opposite is composed of dried pink and blue larkspur flowers, roses, hydrangea and strawflowers, with a single peony at the base of the shape. To make the ring into a heart shape, carefully bend a double copper-wire ring frame into shape at the top and the bottom *(below)*. Now cover the frame with

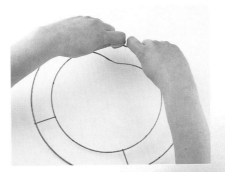

moss, as described in the Techniques section. The flowers are secured in place by pushing their stub wires through the moss and then bending the wires back on themselves.

• You can add another dimension to the table wreath by displaying it with a group of scented candles in toning colours. If you do so, do not leave the lighted candles unattended at any time, or allow them to burn down too low.

> **HINTS**
> Whichever type of base you use, you can attach the flowers to it using a hot glue gun or clear all-purpose adhesive. If you use hot glue, take care not to get any on your fingers, as it can burn. Never leave the appliance unattended when it is plugged into the electricity, and be careful to keep it away from children.

Opposite: Wreaths don't have to be round — just bend a wire ring into the desired shape before covering it with moss, as in this heart-shaped wreath. *For details see Variations.*

BASICALLY FABRIC

In this section, a rich variety of fabrics are used to create exquisite wreaths and a graceful swag. Choose from soft muslin, vivid silk, pink satin, cheerful sprigged prints — or pick a fabric to suit your decor. Each project involves a little sewing, but none involves difficult techniques.

Christmas print wreath • Silk Christmas wreath
Patchwork wreath • Lace and satin ring
Soft muslin swag • Silk heart

CHRISTMAS PRINT WREATH

Here's one festive decoration that can be kept from year to year — a friendly plaited wreath, in which tubes of three Christmas prints are entwined and topped with a padded bow. This wreath will look lovely on an internal door or over the hearth.

1 From each piece of fabric, cut a strip 45 × 6¹/₂in (114 × 17cm). Fold each strip in half lengthwise, with right sides together and raw edges even; pin and stitch a ⁵/₈in (1.5cm) seam along the long edge, forming a tube of fabric. Trim the seam allowance and turn each fabric tube right side out.

2 Fill each fabric tube evenly with wadding (batting) *(below)*, and then pin the ends closed.

3 Holding the three fabric tubes together at one end with a clothespeg (clothespin), plait (braid) the tubes together. Bend the plait into a circle, remove the clothespeg and sew the ends together to form a ring.

4 For the bow, cut one piece of wadding (batting) and two pieces of fabric, each 22 × 6¹/₂in (56 × 17cm).

Place the fabric pieces with right sides together and raw edges even, then lay the wadding on top. Pin and stitch ⁵/₈in (1.5cm) seams down the long edges. Trim the seam allowances and turn right side out.

5 Fold back the raw edges so they just overlap; pin. Work running stitches across the centre *(below)*; draw up into gathers and fasten off.

6 For the bow knot, cut one piece of wadding and two pieces of fabric, each 9¹/₂ × 3in (24 × 7.5cm). Make up the knot piece in the same way as the bow (step 4).

7 Position the bow at the top of the wreath over the sewn ends. Wrap the knot piece tightly around the centre of the bow and the wreath; turn under

the raw edges *(bottom of previous column)* and handsew at the back.

8 Handsew a curtain ring to the back of the wreath at the point where the ends of the knot piece meet *(below)*.

VARIATIONS
• Check out craft fabrics — instead of festive prints you could go for the more homely printed fabrics and have the wreath hanging up in the house all year round.
• Add a small amount of pot-pourri in the bow padding to give a room a fresh fragrance.
• Replace the bow with a large ribbon or fabric rosette or cover the ends with a traditional arrangement of balls and seasonal foliage and flowers.

HINTS
When making up the tubes, check that they are well-filled, as this will produce a really firm wreath which will last longer than one Christmas. Use a thick knitting needle to help push the wadding down the tube.

SILK CHRISTMAS WREATH

*Give a Christmas wreath the star treatment by weaving a thread of gold through
the entwined festive fabrics. A pleated fan made up of both fabrics combined with glittery
ornaments highlights the top of the wreath.*

MATERIALS

*½yd (40cm) each of silk fabric, 45in
(115cm) wide, in 2 colours*

wadding (batting)

*2¼yd (2m) of gold braid, ⅜in (1cm)
wide*

1yd (1m) of gold cord

matching sewing thread

a few glittery Christmas ornaments

*1 curtain ring, ½in (1.3cm) in
diameter*

1 Cut a 40 × 6in (100 × 15cm) strip
from each fabric. Fold each piece
in half lengthwise with right sides
together and raw edges even; stitch a
⅝in (1.5cm) seam along the long edge
of each fabric strip, forming a fabric
tube. Trim the seam allowance to
reduce bulk, and then turn each fabric
tube right side out *(below)*.

2 Fill each fabric tube with wadding
(batting), and then pin the raw ends
of the fabric together.

3 Holding the two fabric tubes
together at one end with a clothespeg (clothespin), twist the tubes tightly
together. Bend them into a circle,
remove the clothespeg and sew the
ends together to form the wreath.

4 Bind the twisted tubes tightly with
gold braid, tucking the raw ends of
the braid inside the twisted section at
the top. If you bind tightly enough, it
will stay in place without being sewn.

5 For the fan piece, cut a 14½ × 9½in
(37 × 24cm) rectangle from each
fabric. Place the two pieces with right
sides together and raw edges even; pin
and stitch a ⅜in (1cm) seam all the way
around, leaving an opening in one side.
Trim the corners *(below)* and turn the
fan piece right side out. Turn in the
edges of the opening and slipstitch
together to close.

6 Run a gathering thread across the
fan piece 3¼in (8cm) from one
short edge *(below)*. Run another
gathering thread 4¼in (11cm) from
the opposite short edge.

7 Wrap the fan piece over the wreath
top with the short edge in front
and the gathering threads lined up. The
portion of the fan piece at the back will
extend about 1¼in (3cm) beyond the
portion in front. Draw up the gathering
threads tightly to form the fan shape,
and fasten off. Sew in place.

8 Handsew a curtain ring to the back
of the wreath for hanging. Fold the
length of cord in half and then tie a
double knot. Handsew it to the top of
the fan. Add glittery ornaments to
decorate the wreath, bending the stems
around the knot in the cord *(below)*.

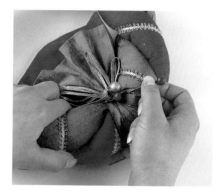

VARIATIONS

• Lengths of bead, pearl or sequin
trim could easily be substituted for the
braid or gold cord.

• This wreath can be made up for
other special occasions. Why not make
it up in silver or gold coloured fabrics
or brocade for special wedding
anniversaries?

• Make up the same idea but in
miniature to use as name plates on the
Christmas table — use a glittery fabric
pen to write the name of the person on
the fan, at the wreath top. And in
miniature, these silk wreaths could
always be used as tree decorations.

PATCHWORK WREATH

Small pieces of toning fabrics were stitched together in a traditional patchwork arrangement to produce this attractive wreath. The dark, muted shades can be changed to bright primary tones to fit in with more modern surroundings.

MATERIALS
$^1/_6$yd (15cm) each of fabric 36in
  (90cm) wide in 2 designs
$^3/_4$yd (70cm) of fabric 36in (90cm)
  wide in a third design
wadding (batting)
$1^3/_4$yd (1.50m) of double satin
  ribbon, $^3/_8$in (1cm) wide
matching sewing thread
1 curtain ring, $^1/_2$in (1.3cm) in
  diameter

1 Using the pattern on page 86, make a template for the patches used for the wreath front. Draw around the template and then carefully cut out four patches from each of two fabrics *(below)*. (The pattern includes seam allowances, so there is no need to add extra for them.)

2 Take two patches — one of each fabric you have cut out — and place the patches with right sides together and raw edges even. Pin and stitch a $^3/_8$in (1cm) seam along one long edge; press the seam open. Repeat for the other six patches.

3 Stitch one pair to another pair along the straight edges, with the fabric alternating, again taking a $^3/_8$in (1cm) seam allowance; press the seam open. Repeat until all the patches are joined into a circle, which will form the wreath front.

4 Using the front as a pattern, cut one piece of wadding (batting) and one piece of the fabric to the same size. Pin and tack (baste) the wadding to the wrong side of the wreath front.

5 For the frill, cut $3^1/_4$in (8cm) wide strips from the third fabric, and join the ends, with right sides together, taking $^3/_8$in (1cm) seams, until the strip is 80in (200cm) long. Stitch the remaining ends together to form a ring, again with a $^3/_8$in (1cm) seam; press the seam open.

6 Fold the frill in half lengthwise, wrong sides together. Divide the frill into quarters, and mark the quarter points. Run two rows of gathering stitches around the frill $^3/_8$in (1cm) from the raw edges.

7 Place the frill on the right side of the patchwork wreath front, with the raw edges of the frill even with the raw outer edges of the wreath front. Match the quarter points of the frill to the centre top, centre base and centre of each side of the wreath, and pin. Draw up the gathers evenly to fit *(below)*.

8 Pin and stitch the frill in place all around the edge, taking a $^3/_8$in (1cm) seam allowance. Be careful to keep the gathers of the frill even and at right angles to the seamline.

9 Place the back over the front with right sides together, covering the frill, and with raw edges even. Pin and stitch around the outer edge. Turn the wreath right side out. Add more wadding to create a rounded effect. Turn in the raw edges around the centre hole; pin and slipstitch together.

10 Cut the ribbon into eight equal pieces and tie each one into a bow. Handsew the bows to the wreath at the outer edge of the seams, next to the frill *(below)*. Handsew a curtain ring to the wrong side of the wreath, at the top, for hanging.

LACE AND SATIN RING

*This well-rounded wreath of pink satin has been decorated with dressmaking
pins. Stitch a pretty lace down one edge of the fabric and wind it around the padded base
before anchoring at intervals with the pearlized pins.*

MATERIALS
*cane wreath, 12in (30cm) in
    diameter
wadding (batting)
strip of bias-cut pink satin 120 × 5in
    (300 × 13cm)
3³/₈yd (3m) of insertion lace
pearl-headed pins
white ready-made ribbon bows
1yd (1m) of ribbon, 1in (2.5cm) wide
1yd (1m) of white sheer ribbon,
    3¹/₂in (9cm) wide
matching sewing thread
1 curtain ring, ¹/₂in (1.3cm) in
    diameter*

1 Cut 4in (10cm) strips of wadding (batting) and wrap them around and around the cane wreath, until it is completely covered. Catch the end in place with a few hand stitches.

2 With raw edges even, pin and stitch the lace to one long edge of the bias satin strip *(below)*.

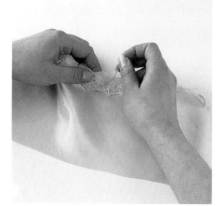

3 Wrap the satin strip around and around the wreath, tucking under the raw edges and securing the fabric in place with pearl-headed pins as you go *(below)*. Decorate the wreath with ready-made ribbon bows.

4 Place the wide ribbon and the narrower ribbon together and tie them into a bow around the top of the wreath *(below)*. Trim the ribbon ends diagonally. Handsew a curtain ring to the back of the wreath for hanging.

VARIATIONS
• Instead of a lace edging, you could make up a self-frill or a contrasting frill and stitch it to the fabric strips before winding them around the ring.
• Glass-headed pins can be matched to the chosen fabric. Those in plain primary colours would look good with ginghams and stripes or pretty sprig prints. These pins also come in deep pastel, pearlized colours which would look electric with striking geometric or shiny, slightly gaudy fabrics. Remember to change the ribbons at the top to go with the new fabrics.
• Plain pins can also be used: team tiny brass-coloured lace pins with beads or sequins before pushing them into place. Or pin through the centre of ribbon roses or buttons — all will hold the bands of fabric securely in place.

HINT
The beauty of this wreath is that it can be made up over any foundation because it is so well wrapped in wadding. Garden centres are a good source of wreath bases as they have various cane and floral foam versions. The cane wreath can be quickly covered and padded to a nice round shape and then the fabric added over the top. As the fabric layers are pinned in place, there is little stitching in this wreath.

Soft Muslin Swag

*Gather up sweeps of muslin over a mirror, bed head or doorway and
decorate each end with clusters of pulled up rosettes of ribbon. Wire-edged ribbon is used for
the caught-up streamers hanging from under each cluster.*

MATERIALS
1²/₃yd (1.50m) sheer muslin
2¹/₄yd (2m) organdie ribbon with
  pull threads, 1¹/₄in (3.5cm) wide,
  in yellow and in white
5yd (4.60m) wire-edged ribbon
  1¹/₄in (3.5cm) wide, in yellow and
  in white
matching sewing thread
2 curtain rings, ¹/₂in (1.3cm) in
  diameter
pearl trim

1 Lay the muslin out flat and,
following the diagram on page 86,
measure and mark out the shape; cut it
out. Turn under and stitch a narrow
hem along both long edges. (There is no
need to hem the ends.)

2 Run a line of gathering stitches
across each end. Draw up the
gathers and fasten off.

3 To make two pompons out of the
yellow organdie ribbon and two
out of the white, cut a 40in (100cm)
length of ribbon for each pompon,
then form the pompon by pulling up
the threads that run through the
ribbon along the edges *(below)*; tie off.

4 Make up three bows in yellow and
three in white. For each bow, cut an
18in (45cm) length of wire-edged
ribbon. Turn in the raw ends so that
they meet in the centre, forming a bow
shape; twist them together. Cut two
62in (155cm) lengths of wire-edged
ribbon, in each colour, for the long ties.

5 Lay three bows on top of one
another, alternating the colours.
Handsew in place, and sew the centre of
one white and one yellow tie behind
the three bows *(below)*.

6 Handsew the bows to one gathered
end of the swag. Handsew two
pompons over the bow. Repeat for the
other three bows and other two
pompons, sewing them to the other
end of the swag *(top of next column)*.

7 Handsew a curtain ring behind
each arrangement. Roll up the long
ties then pull the centres to create curls.

8 Handsew lengths of pearl trim
across the folds of the swag, holding
them with a few stitches behind the
arrangements at each end *(below)*.

*Right:
The ribbon
streamers
hanging from
bows form the
"drops", or
"cascades" of
the muslin
swag.*

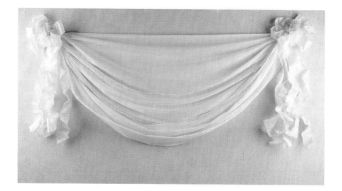

SILK HEART

No one could resist being your valentine if you presented them with this elaborate wreath cardboard. A shaped cardboard mount is padded and covered in shiny red silk, then jewels of all shapes and sizes, particularly different hearts, are dotted over the front.

MATERIALS
thick cardboard
wadding (batting)
³/₅yd (50cm) red silk fabric, 55in (140cm) wide
matching sewing thread
sequins, jewels and feathers
4yd (3.60m) tartan ribbon, 1¹/₂in (3.8cm wide)
pearl trim
fabric glue
curtain ring, ¹/₂in (1.3cm) in diameter

1 On a photocopier, enlarge the heart pattern on page 86 by 200 percent (or enlarge it by using a grid). Transfer the pattern to cardboard, and cut out. Cut 2in (5cm) wide strips of wadding (batting) and bind all around the cardboard heart *(below)*.

2 Measure the distance all around the wrapped cardboard heart, and also the width. Make up a strip of red silk to twice the width of the heart plus 1¹/₄in (3cm), and a length of twice the distance around the heart.

3 With the right side out, wrap the fabric strip around the heart shape. As you go, turn under the raw edges on the outer edge, and pin together *(below)*. Work a running stitch along the folded edges, gently gathering up the fabric around the padded heart.

4 Where the raw edges meet at the ends of the strip, turn under one raw edge and overlap the opposite one.

5 Stick sequins and glass "jewels" all over the front of the fabric heart using fabric glue.

6 Tie a bow in the centre of the ribbon. Handsew it to the centre top of the heart. Take the ends behind the side edges and handsew in place.

7 Following the instructions for making ribbon roses on page 70 (steps 4-5), make three roses from the tartan ribbon *(below)* and sew them to the bow.

8 Wrap the pearl trim around the heart, fastening the ends in place. Tuck feathers into the ribbon knot.

9 Handsew a curtain ring to the centre top of the wrong side of the heart, for hanging.

HINTS
One great advantage of wreaths is that they require only a nominal amount of fabric, so you can afford to splash out on an expensive designer fabric or piece of antique lace or silk, as in this heart wreath.

Because only a little is needed, remnants purchased from fabric stores can be used. Alternatively, when you buy some fabric for a dress or a furnishing project, buy a little extra to turn into a wreath or swag.

Closely woven fabrics that do not fray are easiest to sew and will give a good result. Non-fraying fabrics like felt and net are useful, especially for binding and bow-making. If you use a printed fabric or a checked or striped weave, avoid anything too large in scale. Sprigs and other small prints will look best.

Ribbons and braids come in all widths and colours, so it is easy to find a good match for your particular fabric. Look beyond the plain ones — there are also printed, jacquard and decoratively edged ribbons to be found. Lace trimming can have either a single edge for inserting into a seam, or a finished edge on both sides.

ALL THE TRIMMINGS

*Although the wreaths and garland in this section are
mainly based on fabric, it is the trimmings that make them
distinctive, ranging from raffia and hessian, to butterflies
and pearls. Follow the instructions exactly, or simply use them as a
starting point for your own ideas and combinations.*

Wedding wreath • Crepe paper wreath • Ribbon ring
Shaker garland • Shaker circle • Button ring
Natural wreath • Sewing wreath • Appliqué butterfly ring

WEDDING WREATH

*If you've no time to make a traditional wedding wreath, why not quickly run
up this one using kitchen foil and net? The fabric is bunched up and tied with lengths of
beads and ribbon ties and covered with celebratory cake decorations.*

MATERIALS
*dry foam wreath base, 12in (30cm)
    in diameter*
aluminium foil
*60 × 12in (150 × 30cm) piece of
    white net*
*47 × 16in (120 × 40cm) piece of
    pink net*
*2³/₄yd (2.50m) of silver Russia braid
    (soutache braid)*
*2³/₄yd (2.50m) of pink ribbon, ¹/₈in
    (3mm) wide*
*2³/₄yd (2.50m) of fine dark pink
    braid*
pearl trim
small ready-made pink roses
pink net
small white plastic doves
silver glitter glue pen
silver horseshoes
*1 curtain ring, ¹/₂in (1.3cm) in
    diameter*

1 Cut one piece of aluminium foil
measuring 40 × 8¹/₂in (100 × 22cm).
Wrap the piece of foil around the foam
wreath base, bunching it up to create a
wrinkled effect *(below)*. Overlap the
raw edges of the foil and make sure that
it is tightly wrapped.

2 Fold the piece of white net in half
around the wreath base, enclosing it
between the two layers of fabric. Turn in
the raw edges by ³/₈in (1mm) and pin
together all around the inner edge
(below). Overlap the raw ends at the top.

3 Cut the silver braid, pink ribbon
and pink braid into five 20in
(50cm) lengths of each. Tie one length
of each together tightly around the net-
covered wreath at the base. Repeat twice
on each side so that the ribbons are
evenly spaced *(below)*. Remove the pins
as you tie the knots. Bunch up the net
evenly between the ties.

4 Pin a ready-made rose through the
centre of each tie into the foam.
Trim the tie ends diagonally.

5 Wind pearl trim around the wreath
in a criss-cross fashion *(below)*. This
will help to hold the net in place, and
also the wedding decorations.

6 Wind the pink net around the
centre top of the wreath, tying it in
a big bow *(below)*. Cut the ends
diagonally. *(Continued on page 69)*

7 Use glitter glue to paint around the edges of the tail and wings of each dove *(below)*; leave to dry.

8 Add the doves and the silver horsehoe decorations, sliding them under the pearl trim *(below)*.

9 Handsew a curtain ring to the centre top of the wreath at the back to use for hanging.

VARIATION

• The same techniques can be used for other celebration rings. Instead of foil and net, you could wrap crepe paper around the base *(below)* as in the **crepe paper wreath** in the photograph. Cut it to a length of one and a half times the wreath circumference, and the width plus $^3/_4$in (2cm), and then turn under

the long edges by $^3/_8$in (1cm). Tie the crepe paper in place with narrow satin ribbon and bunch it up between the ribbons, as for the main project. You could then bind the wreath with pearl trim or ribbon-threaded lace *(below)*. Ribbon roses are appropriate decoration on a variety of occasions.

Opposite: Crepe paper is used instead of foil and net for this delightful crepe paper wreath, *illustrating the wide range of materials that can be used. For details see Variation.*

RIBBON RING

*Ribbon flowers are always popular and these are no exception — built up from
short lengths of ribbon, they are sewn close together over a plain fabric-covered base to create
a dramatic and colourful wreath.*

MATERIALS
thick cardboard
wadding (batting)
*⁵/₈yd (60cm) of plain green fabric,
36in (90cm) wide*
*3³/₈yd (3m) each of green, red and
tartan ribbons, 3in (7.5cm) wide*
*6³/₄ yd (6.10m) of yellow ribbon,
1¹/₂in (3.8cm) wide*
matching sewing thread
stub wires
fine silver floral wire
green floral tape
*1 curtain ring, ¹/₂in (1.3cm) in
diameter*

1 Make a padded covered cardboard wreath *(below)* in the same way as for the Appliqué Butterfly Wreath on page 82 (steps 1 and 2).

2 Cover it with fabric in the same way as for that wreath (steps 3, 9 and 10), omitting the frill, and gently pleating the fabric in the centre of the wreath instead of gathering it up.

3 Use the "shell" pattern shown on page 86 to make a template. Draw around the template and cut out 14 shell shapes from the red, green and tartan ribbons. To create each shell, work a row of gathering stitches down one side, across the short base and up the other side, ¹/₄in (6mm) from the edge. Draw up the thread to make each piece into a shell *(below)*, and wind the thread around the base to fasten off.

4 To make a yellow rose, cut a 32in (80cm) length of yellow ribbon. Cut a 4in (10cm) length of stub wire and bend over the end to form a loop. Fold one end of the ribbon over the wire loop and bind around it with fine wire. Turn the stub wire around a few times to create the rose centre, and bind around it with fine wire.

5 Now take the ribbon end and diagonally fold it, turning the rose at the same time; bind around the stem. Keep folding and turning the rose to create the petals. Bind around the stem with the fine wire, then bring the end down to the base and bind tightly. Cover the stem with green floral tape. Make five more roses in the same way *(top of next column)*.

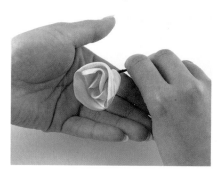

6 Handsew the ribbon shells to the fabric-covered wreath, beginning on either side of centre top and over-lapping the shells. Alternate the colours as you work around to the centre of the wreath base. Handsew yellow ribbon roses among the shells.

7 Cut a 30in (76cm) length of yellow ribbon and tie it into a generous bow, with long tails. Handsew the bow to the wreath *(below)*.

8 Handsew a curtain ring to the centre top of the wreath on the wrong side, for hanging.

VARIATION
• Instead of bright, contrasting colours, combine softly toning ribbons.

SHAKER GARLAND

Following the traditional style of the Shakers, this garland features simple shapes
in plain fabrics mixed with natural ears of wheat. Hang it over a doorway or draped across
the fireplace during the summer months.

1 Trace the patterns for the heart front and back and the bell front/back, which are shown on page 87, to make templates. Draw around the templates and cut out one pair of heart back pieces, one heart front and two bells from each of the checked fabrics. (The patterns include seam allowances, so there is no need to add extra.)

2 From the interlining, cut three hearts and three bells. Trim off ³/₈in (1cm) all around each. Using pinking shears, cut six 2in (5cm) squares of calico (unbleached muslin).

3 Centre a heart-shaped piece of the interlining on the wrong side of each heart front. Position a calico square in the centre of the right side of each

heart front. Pin and topstitch each calico square in place, through all three layers (calico, checked fabric and interlining), leaving a small opening at the top *(bottom of previous column)*. Do the same for the three bell fronts.

4 Place the pair of heart back pieces in each colour together. On each pair, pin and stitch a ⁵/₈in (1.5cm) seam along the long edge *(below)*, leaving an opening in the centre; press the seam open.

5 Place a heart front and a heart back with right sides together; pin and stitch them together all around, taking a ³/₈in (1cm) seam. Trim the seam allowance, and turn right side out through the opening in the centre back

seam *(bottom of previous column)*. Turn in the opening edges; slipstitch.

6 Place the bells together in pairs of one front and one back for each colour, with right sides together and raw edges even. Pin and stitch all around, leaving an opening in the base. Trim the seam allowance and turn right side out through the opening. Turn in the opening edges and slipstitch to close.

7 Cut six 8in (20cm) lengths of ribbon. Handsew the centre of one length of ribbon to the centre top of a shape. Cut the ribbon ends diagonally. Repeat for all the shapes.

8 Cut six small bunches of wheat and slide one into the calico pocket on each shape *(below)*.

9 Tie the shapes to the piping cord at regular intervals, finishing with a bow. At each end of the garland tie the cord around a bundle of wheat *(top of first column, page 75)* and into loops for hanging. *(Continued on page 75)*

• The same checked hearts can be stuffed and then used to make the **Shaker circle** in the photograph opposite. Use the heart patterns on page 87 to cut two fronts and two pairs of backs from each of the three Shaker-type checked fabrics. Make up the hearts in the same way as for the garland (steps 4 and 5), omitting the calico pockets and interlining, and filling them with kapok *(below)* or other stuffing before slipstitching the opening closed.

Sew a ³/₄in (20mm) diameter blue wooden bead between each pair of hearts near the base. Handsew a ¹/₂in (1.3cm) curtain ring to the wrong side at the top of one heart, for hanging.

VARIATIONS
• Instead of putting little pockets on the fronts of the hearts, just topstitch a square of loosely woven hessian (burlap), ³/₈in (1cm) from the outer edge. Then fray the edges of the square up to the stitching line.
• If you like the pocket idea, take out the corn and add tiny dried flowers.
• Make a garland for a special occasion and fill the pockets with little sweets for the children.
• Garden twine can be used instead of jumbo cord for the actual garland length on which the hearts are tied. If the twine seems thin, plait double strands together. Garden twine comes in natural as well as green, so the colours should blend well together.

Attach lengths of narrow ribbon to the padded hearts *(below)* in the same way as for the garland (step 7), but tie them in bows.

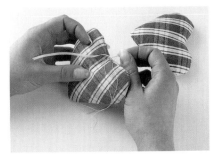

Opposite: The Shaker-type checked fabric used for the garland is also used for these hearts, which are sewn together to make a Shaker circle. Wooden beads echo the simple, natural look. For details see Variations.

Sew the hearts together in a circle. with a ⁵/₈in (15mm) diameter natural-coloured wooden bead between them *(top of next column).*

75

BUTTON RING

Any collection of buttons has a certain fascination, so here's how to put your old buttons to good use. All different shapes and sizes sit happily side-by-side in this cheerful arrangement — just sew them in position.

MATERIALS
cardboard
³/₈yd (40cm) green silk fabric
curtain interlining or, if unavailable, wadding (batting)
tissue paper
assorted buttons in tones of white and ecru and in different sizes
spray glue
small ribbon roses
matching sewing thread
piece of felt for backing
masking tape
small amount of ribbon, ³/₄in (2cm) wide, for hanging loop
pair of compasses

1 On cardboard draw a circle 10in (25cm) in diameter. With a pair of compasses, draw a 4in (10cm) circle in the centre. Cut out.

2 Cut out a 12¹/₂in (32cm) square of fabric, and another of interlining. Place the interlining on the wrong side of the fabric and tack (baste) together.

3 Cut a square of tissue paper to a similar size as the fabric. Mark a 10in (25cm) circle on the tissue paper.

Mark three more circles, with diameters of 3¹/₂in (9cm), 4³/₄in (12cm) and 6in (15cm), all within the main circle and with the same centre.

4 Lay the tissue paper over the right side of the fabric, and pin in place. Work a row of small tacking stitches around the marked lines on the tissue paper, through all layers *(below)*. Gently tear away the tissue paper, leaving the stitching on the fabric.

5 Draw around the cardboard circle onto a piece of paper. Lay out the buttons in a haphazard arrangement inside this marked outline and move them around until you are happy with the way they look.

6 Transferring the buttons to the fabric one at a time, handsew them in place, positioning the first ones over the inner marked line *(top of next column)*; there is no need to fasten off after each button. Sew on the second row of buttons along the second marked line. Now sew on the remaining rounds of buttons, butting the edges together. Remove the tacking stitches.

7 Use spray glue to stick the fabric over the cardboard circle. Trim the edges and turn the fabric to the wrong side around the outer edge; tape it in place. Snip into the fabric around the inner edge, then turn this to the wrong side of the ring; tape in place.

8 Remove the leaves from the ribbon roses. Handsew the roses around the inner edge of the ring *(below)*.

9 Cut a 3¹/₂in (9cm) length of ribbon: fold it in half and handsew to the wrong side at the top to form a loop which projects beyond the edge.

10 Lay the ring on a piece of felt and mark around the edge. Using pinking shears, carefully cut out the felt so that it is ¹/₄in (6mm) smaller all around. Stick the felt ring over the wrong side of the button wreath.

NATURAL WREATH

*Lengths of hessian (burlap) roughly cut so that they fray, then wrapped around a
ring of cane, provide an appropriate base for tiny hanging pots filled with dried flowers and
grasses. Use natural and synthetic raffia to bind the wreath together.*

MATERIALS
*cane wreath, 12in (30cm) in
   diameter
5 tiny flower pots
hessian (burlap)
shiny golden-brown synthetic raffia
fine paper ribbon
natural raffia
dried flowers and sweetcorn cobs
PVA (white) glue
fennel seeds
small amount of dry floral foam*

1 Cut the hessian (burlap) into 2½in (6.5cm) wide strips; fray the edges for ⅜in (1cm) on each side *(below)*.

2 Fold the strips in half lengthwise so the frayed edges are uneven; wind them around the wreath *(below)*. Slot the ends into the wreath to fasten off.

3 Wind the golden-brown synthetic raffia around the wreath over the hessian *(below)*.

4 Cut 22in (56cm) lengths of fine paper ribbon. Tie them in pairs around the wreath and curl up the ends, using the scissors blade *(below)*.

5 Cut three 40in (100cm) lengths of natural raffia. Plait (braid) the lengths of raffia together and then wind them around the wreath between the hessian strips.

6 Paint the rim of each flower pot with PVA (white) glue, then roll the rim in fennel seeds; leave to dry *(below)*.

7 Cut 15 lengths of natural raffia, each 20in (50cm) long. Plait them together to make five plaits. Thread each plait through a flower pot. Use the plaits to tie the flower pots around the wreath, spacing them equally but leaving a gap at the top.

8 Cut five small pieces of dry floral foam and push one of them down inside each of the flower pots; glue in place. Cut flower heads and push them inside each pot.

9 Cut a 47 × 2½in (120 × 6.5cm) strip of hessian, and fray both long edges as in step 1. Wrap the strip around the centre top of the wreath and tie it into a bow. Fray the ends, insert the stems of two dried flowers into the knot, and tie synthetic raffia around the bow, curling the ends.

10 Hang the wreath with another length of natural raffia, knotted securely through the cane wreath at the top centre of the back.

SEWING WREATH

Ideal for the sewing enthusiast, this wreath mixes areas of pinked-edged fabric
squares with the knick-knacks always needed within easy reach by the happy stitcher. The
base is non-fraying felt, which provides a firm and colourful background.

MATERIALS
polystyrene (foam) ring, 12in (30cm)
in diameter
wadding (batting)
blue felt
small amounts of sprig print fabrics
dressmaking pins
pinking shears
matching sewing thread
fusible web
large safety pin
items to put on wreath, such as small
scissors, a tape measure, needles, a
dressmaker's pencil, a needle
threader, tailor's chalk
curtain ring, ¹/₂in (1.3cm) in
diameter, for hanging

1 Cut 2in (5cm) wide strips of wadding (batting) and bind the polystyrene (foam) ring with them, just overlapping the edges.

2 Cut 2in (5cm) wide strips of felt. Bind them around the ring over the wadding *(below)*, making sure that the overlapping joins are in different positions from the wadding overlaps. Secure the ends of strips with pins.

3 Mark out five evenly spaced areas on the wreath. Cut 1¹/₂in (4cm) squares from the print fabrics using pinking shears. Fold each square into quarters and pin the corner into the felt-covered wreath, so that the fabric squares are clustered in the marked areas. Use your fingers to open out the folded squares. Keep adding the squares till the clusters are fairly bushy *(below)*.

4 Cut two pieces of sprig print fabric 4 × 2³/₄in (10 × 7cm). Iron fusible web to the wrong side of one fabric piece, following the manufacturer's instructions. Peel off the backing, and bond it to the wrong side of the second fabric piece.

5 Using pinking shears, cut out one piece 3¹/₂ × 2¹/₄in (9 × 6cm) from the bonded fabrics. Cut one piece of felt slightly smaller, using pinking shears.

6 Position the felt on top of the bonded fabric and stitch down the centre. Fold it in half (like a book) to form a needle case and pin this into one of the gaps on the ring.

7 Bond together two 5¹/₄in (14cm) squares of fabric as in step 4. Draw up the pattern for the scissors case from the template on page 85. Cut out two scissors case pieces from the bonded fabric *(top of next column)*.

8 Place the two pieces together, and turn under the top triangular portion of one piece. Pin and stitch the sides. Pin the scissors case into one of the gaps on the ring.

9 Pin safety pins into another gap, and push dressmaking pins into one of the remaining gaps.

10 Measure around the ring at the top. Cut a strip of felt with the pinking shears to this length plus 4in (10cm) and to a width of 2in (5cm). Using pinking shears, create a fringed effect at both ends of the felt strip by making 1¹/₂in (4cm) cuts of the felt strip ¹/₂in (1.3cm) apart.

12 Fold this piece in half, angling the two halves so the side edges are not even, and position it at the top of the wreath. Fasten the ends together with a large safety pin.

13 Wrap the tape measure around the ring, tucking the ends out of sight. Sew a curtain ring on the back at the top, for hanging. Add any other sewing accessories you are including.

APPLIQUÉ BUTTERFLY RING

*For this lovely wreath, you just cut out simple butterfly shapes, layer them
together with net, then decorate with machine stitching before fixing them to a wreath of
flowers. Use pastel shades or change the colours to suit its location.*

1 Lay a plate that is approximately
10$^1/_2$in (27cm) in diameter on the
cardboard. Mark around the edge. Mark
the centre of the circle. Position a plate
or bowl that is about 5in (13cm) in
diameter over the centre, and mark
around the edge. Carefully cut out the
resulting ring, which should be
approximately 2$^3/_4$in (7cm) wide
between the inner and outer edges.

2 Using the cardboard as a template,
cut out three pieces of wadding
(batting). Glue one piece of wadding to
one side of the cardboard ring, for the
front. Place the remaining wadding
pieces on each side. Oversew (overcast)
the outer and inner edges of the layers
of wadding together enclosing the
cardboard ring *(top of next column).*

3 Measure around the outer edge of
the padded ring. Measure the width
of the ring (the distance from the outer
edge to the inner edge). Cut two pieces
of silk fabric and one piece of lace fabric
to these dimensions plus 1$^1/_4$in (3cm)
each way for seam allowances.

4 With right sides together and raw
edges even, pin the ends of one strip
together; stitch a $^5/_8$in (1.5cm) seam and
press the seam open, forming a ring.
Repeat for the other two strips.

5 Place the lace ring over the right
side of one silk ring; pin and tack
(baste) the two rings together. Fold into
quarters, and mark the quarter points.

6 To make the frill, cut and join
5$^1/_2$in- (14cm-) wide silk strips until
you have a continuous strip that is
twice the circumference of the ring.

7 Pin and stitch the frill into a ring as
in step 4, pressing the seam open.
Fold the frill in half, with wrong sides
together and raw edges even. Now run
a line of gathering stitches all around,
$^3/_8$in (1cm) from the raw edges. Divide
the frill into quarters, marking the
quarter points.

8 Position the frill on the right side of
the lace ring, around the outer edge,
matching the quarter points. Draw up
the gathers of the frill evenly to fit; pin
and tack (baste) the frill in place along
the gathering line.

9 Place the second silk ring on the
lace ring with right sides together;
pin and stitch a $^5/_8$in (1.5cm) seam all
around the outer edge. Trim the seam
allowance, and turn right side out.

10 Wrap the fabric cover around
the padded cardboard wreath.
Turn under the raw inner edges of both
front and back and run a line of
gathering stitches around these folded
edges. Draw up the gathering threads
evenly, adjusting the fabric, and fasten
off. Slipstitch the gathered edges
together *(below).*

11 Use the patterns on page 84-5 to
make templates for the two
butterfly shapes. Mark four of each
shape on fusible web. Following the
manufacturer's instructions, iron the
fusible web onto one layer of cotton
fabric, making two of each shape in
green and two of each in yellow.
Carefully cut them out.

12 Position two ready-made flower stamens at the top of each head as antennae, and then fuse the butterfly shape onto a second layer of fabric, sandwiching the antennae between the two layers. Wind gold thread onto the sewing machine spool. Using a close zigzag stitch (satin stitch) on the machine, sew around the wings only.

13 Place the butterfly on two layers of net in the same colour as the cotton, and zigzag stitch around the body only. Cut out the butterfly through all layers *(below)*.

14 For each of the three ribbon lilies, cut five 5½in (14cm) lengths of cream satin ribbon. Fold in the raw edges of each length of ribbon so that they meet in the centre, and pin them in place.

15 Make up a stamen by threading one gold bugle, one pearl and a second gold bugle onto a length of fine wire *(top of next column)*; twist the ends together. Make nine stamens in all.

16 Wrap the petals of a lily around three stamens and attach the lily to a stub wire with fine floral wire wrapped around the base *(below)*. Cover with white tape, to hold.

17 Handsew the eight butterflies around the wreath *(below)*. Handsew the three lilies in a cluster at the bottom. Handsew a curtain ring to the centre top of the wrong side of the wreath, for hanging.

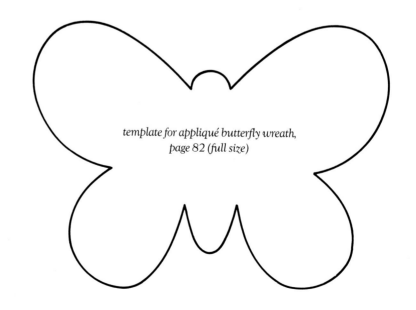

template for appliqué butterfly wreath, page 82 (full size)

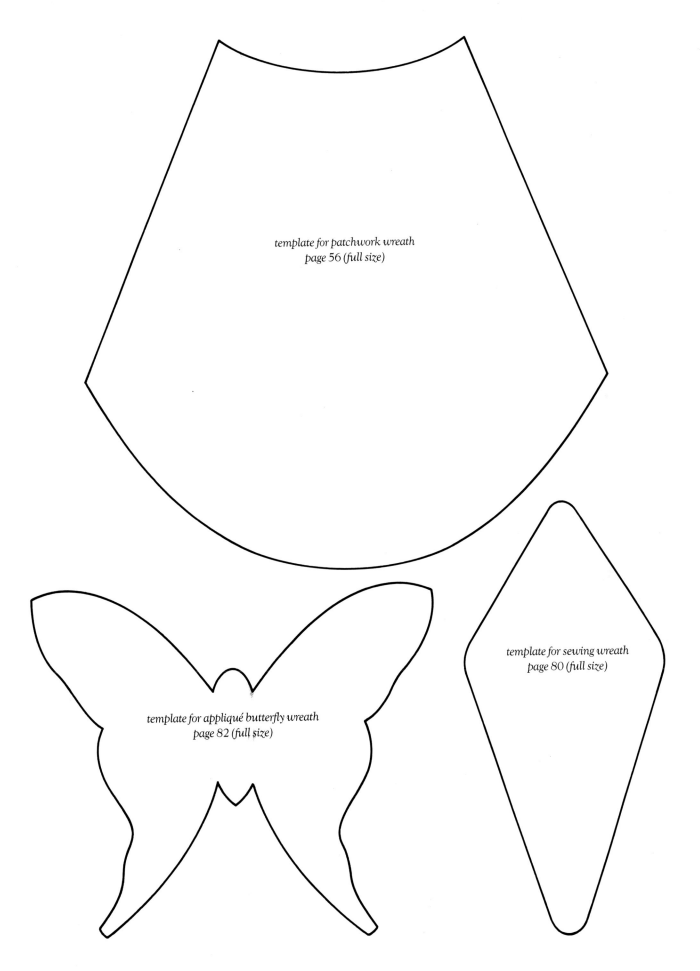

template for patchwork wreath
page 56 (full size)

template for sewing wreath
page 80 (full size)

template for appliqué butterfly wreath
page 82 (full size)

85

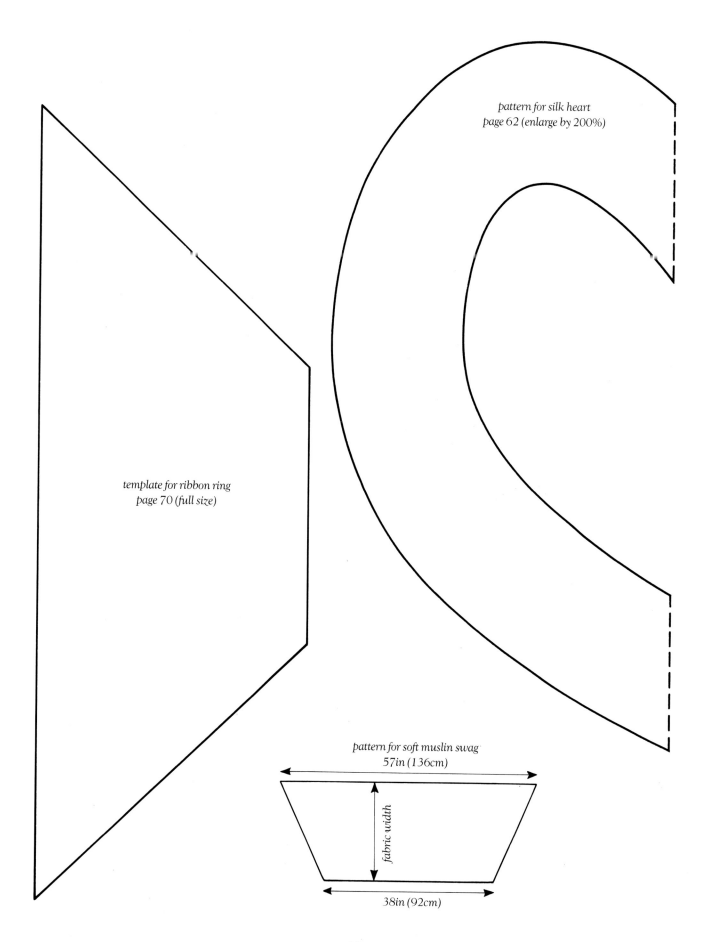

pattern for silk heart
page 62 (enlarge by 200%)

template for ribbon ring
page 70 (full size)

pattern for soft muslin swag
57in (136cm)

fabric width

38in (92cm)

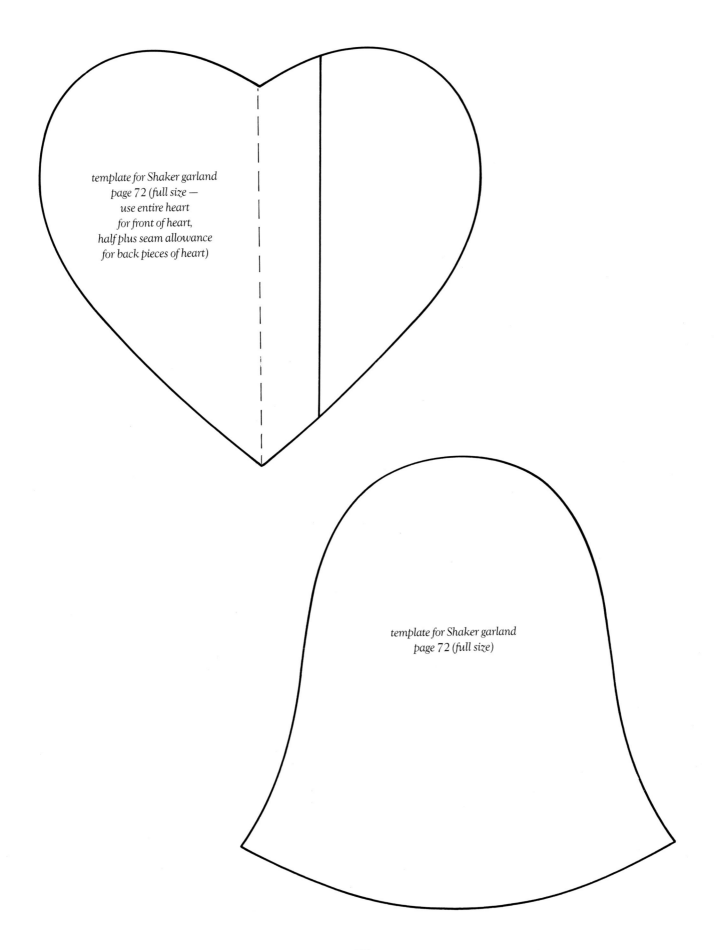

template for Shaker garland
page 72 (full size —
use entire heart
for front of heart,
half plus seam allowance
for back pieces of heart)

template for Shaker garland
page 72 (full size)

TECHNIQUES

The joy of making swags, wreaths and garlands is that it is possible to put together beautiful, highly individual creations very easily. There are no particular skills required, and the techniques are not difficult to learn.

In this section you will find a selection of simple, basic techniques that will be useful not only for the projects in this book but also for your own designs. They include techniques for making and covering a variety of wreath and garland bases, preparing and looking after the fresh and dried flowers used in them, making hanging loops for them and making bows. Basic techniques for sewing fabric wreaths are also covered, including hand stitches, machine-stitched seams, mitring, corners and how to finish edges using bias binding. Learn these few basic techniques and you will soon discover the pleasure of making your own swags, wreaths and garlands.

WREATH BASES

Wreath bases fall into two broad categories: those made from natural stems such as willow, vine, clematis or dried grasses, all of which are attractive enough to form part of the design, and those made of foam or wire, which need to be completely concealed.

Copper wire ring frames are available in two sizes: 10in (25cm) and 12in (30cm). Made of two concentric wire rings joined by wire spokes, they can be covered with dry moss or hay, blocks of floral foam or paper ribbon before being decorated.

Covering a wire ring with moss

Copper wire ring frames, which are made of two concentric wire rings joined by wire spokes, can be covered with dry moss before being decorated. If preferred, hay can be substituted for the moss.

Tie fine silver floral wire or green garden twine to the outer ring of a wire ring frame. Take up handfuls of dry moss and pack it between the two rings. Bind it securely as you go, pulling the wire or twine taut so it is concealed within the depth of moss *(below)*.

Continue binding on more moss in a thick layer until the ring is covered. Fasten off the binding material.

Covering a wire ring with foam

If you fill in the gaps between the two wire circles with pieces of dry or absorbent foam instead of moss, you will have an improvised but practical stem-holder to use with dried or fresh plant materials.

Cut small rectangular blocks of foam about 2in (5cm) deep. In you are using soaked absorbent foam, wrap the block closely with clingfilm (plastic wrap) or

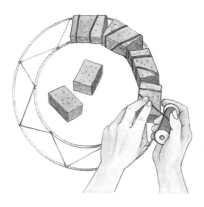

foil to contain the moisture and protect the wall or table surface.

Arrange the blocks around the wire ring frame and bind them securely in place with green garden twine. It does not matter if they do not fit exactly; a few gaps are acceptable *(bottom of previous column)*.

Covering a wire ring with paper ribbon

Creating a hoop of paper ribbon in this way enables you to transform a utilitarian item into one that is decorative and colourful. Choose the colour of the binding ribbon to tone with the dried flowers you plan for the decoration, and finish the design with a flat or rounded paper-ribbon bow.

Cut off a length of paper ribbon and unfurl it. Wrap one edge of the ribbon over the outer ring of the wire ring frame and bind the ribbon around and around, overlapping each layer. Join on more strips if necessary. When the ring is covered, glue the end of the ribbon at the back.

Making a foam circle

If you do not have a pre-formed foam ring, you can easily make one to support flower stems for a table decoration. Use absorbent stem-holding foam for fresh flowers, and dry foam for dried material.

Place a small, shallow dish in the centre of a large, flat plate and measure the distance between the rim of the dish and that of the plate. Cut a block of foam into slices the length of that measurement, and 1 1/4in (3cm) thick. Cut each slice in half lengthwise and trim off two corners. Position the slices around the edge of the plate, with the cut corners inwards.

Position more foam slices to fill the space. Tie a piece of green garden twine or thin string around the outside, to keep the foam in place *(below)*.

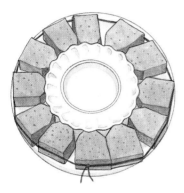

Covering a foam ring with moss
Foam never looks good showing through, whereas moss does. Covering a pre-formed ring of dry or absorbent foam with a thin layer of moss (or, if you prefer, hay) allows you to compose a decoration in which areas of the wreath base may be left on view.

Cut medium-gauge stub wires in half with wire cutters and bend each one into a U-shape.

Take small handfuls of dry moss or hay, spread it thinly over a small area of the foam ring and secure it at intervals with the bent wires *(below)*. Continue around the ring until it is covered.

Making a twig wreath base
If you wish to create your own twig wreath base, use supple twigs such as willow, vine, honeysuckle, clematis, birch, wisteria, or actinidia.

Sort the stems and select the longest ones. If they have become dry and stiff, soak them in a trough of water.

Bend one twig into a circle, then slightly overlap its ends and bind them together with fine silver floral wire or green garden twine. Twist a second and then a third twig around the first, tucking in the ends securely.

Continue adding twigs in this way until the wreath base is the thickness you want. Take another long twig, tuck in one end and use it to bind over and over the ring *(below)*. Join in a second binding twig if necessary, and conceal the ends. Cut off and discard the holding wire or twine.

Making a grassy wreath base
A direct descendant of the stem circlets that country children made in summer, this less substantial base is made from long, supple stems, such as grass, reeds, rushes, weeping willow, bryony or sheep's parsley. It can be decorated with lightweight fresh or dried flowers, or with foliage, small shells or even feathers.

Sort out the stems and discard any short ones. Gather them into a thick bundle, bind green twine around them at one end and knot it securely.

Bind the stems into a tight rope, pulling the twine taut and keeping it as even as possible *(below)*. Overlap the ends to form a ring, bind them securely and fasten off the twine.

GARLAND BASES
Garlands and swags are traditionally composed on cores of twisted stems, rope or plaited straw. Alternatively, a base that provides a water supply can be constructed using floral foam.

Making a grassy garland base
You can make a garland base in a similar way to the method used to make a grassy wreath base, joining in more and more clusters of grassy stems until the natural stem "rope" is the length you require. A natural core like this is good-looking enough to be allowed to show under the decoration.

Making a hay rope
Another attractive option is a rope made of hay, which can be used for draped garlands and swags that are to be decorated with fresh or dried plant materials. Make a slightly thicker version as the base for a vertical swag.

Take a large handful of dry, sweet-smelling hay and form it into a long sausage shape. Wrap green garden twine or thin string around one end,

tie it securely and bind it around and around the hay *(above)*.

Add more and more hay to extend the elongated roll, packing it tightly so that it holds its shape. Bind the "rope" securely, leaving no more than ¹/₂in (1.3cm) between each twist of the binding. When you have the length you need, fasten off the twine securely.

Covering a rope with hay

A rope covered with hay has more substance than one actually made from hay and can support heavier decorative materials, such as fruits and large cones. Like the hay rope, it looks fine if it shows under the decoration. You can use sphagnum moss instead of hay if you prefer.

Take a handful of dry hay (or sphagnum moss) and wrap it around one end of a length of rope. Wind green garden twine or thin string around the hay, knot it tightly and bind it over and around the rope.

Add more handfuls of hay along the length of the rope, pulling the twine taut *(top of next column)*. Fasten it off securely at the end.

Making a foam garland core

Sometimes a garland has to be assembled a day or more before an event, or it may have to look its best over several days of, say, a festival. To keep the flowers and foliage looking fresh, it is advisable to construct a core that provides a moisture source. Blocks of soaked floral foam wrapped in clingfilm (plastic wrap) — to protect the wall or tablecloth from seepage — and then in chicken wire can be wired together, like links of a chain. This core can be made several days before you need to use it, as the foam will stay moist inside the wrapping.

Cut the absorbent foam into blocks, about 3in × 2in × 2in (7.5cm × 5cm × 5cm), or as appropriate to the scale of the garland. Soak the foam thoroughly.

Wrap each foam block closely in clingfilm, and then in chicken wire, folding the wire over like a neatly wrapped parcel.

Bend medium-gauge stub wires in half and use them to link the wire-covered blocks together into a continuous chain *(below)*.

MAKING A HANGING LOOP
You may be able to rest a wall wreath on a peg or hook, or it may be necessary to make a hanging loop. One way to make this is by twisting a supple twig into a loop shape and inserting and securing the ends. Alternatively, you can use a loop of wire, as shown here, covering it with a material appropriate to the wreath decoration, such as gutta-percha (floral) tape, raffia, ribbon or paper ribbon. Wire loops are also suitable for garlands and swags.

Bind a medium-gauge stub wire with the appropriate material and secure it at each end.

Push the wire ends into the wreath base and bend them back to secure them *(below)*. If possible, arrange the decorative materials so that the hook, even if it is covered in a "sympathetic" material, is concealed.

MAKING THE MOST OF FLOWERS
Whether you are composing a fresh-flower table ring or a leafy garland decorated with dainty flower posies, it is important to follow a few basic guidelines to keep your designs looking their best. Here are some pointers to help you.

Fresh flowers
Gather or buy all plant materials in the peak of condition. Do not be tempted to use foliage or flowers that are starting

to fade or wilt; they will only shorten the life of your arrangement.

Recut all stem ends at a sharp angle, using sharp pruning shears or floral scissors. Scrape off the bark for about 2in (5cm) from the ends of woody stems such as holly, eucalyptus and fruit blossom and slit the ends with a sharp knife, or lightly crush the stem ends with a small hammer. This will help them take up water more readily before they are arranged in foam, or without a moisture source.

As soon as you have recut and treated the stem ends, put all fresh plant materials into a deep container of tepid — not cold — water. Leave them in a cool place, away from direct sunlight, for several hours or overnight. This conditioning treatment significantly extends the "vase life" of all fresh flowers and foliage.

When fresh flowers are to be arranged without a moisture source, as they may be when they are used to decorate a foliage garland, leave them in water for as long as possible. Make up posies, bind the stems and leave them in water until just before the event. Make the task of attaching flowers one of the last in your schedule.

Spray all fresh-flower decorations with a fine spray of cool water, and do so at frequent intervals in hot or humid conditions.

Whenever possible, position fresh-flower decorations away from direct heat or sunlight and, if it is practicable, remove them from a heated room overnight.

Keep absorbent foam permanently moist by spraying or lightly watering it every day. Remember to place a decoration such as a fresh-flower wreath on a moisture-proof surface before doing so.

When a decoration composed on absorbent foam eventually fades, you may be able to reuse the foam for future designs. Remove the faded materials, pick out any loose pieces of stem and resoak the foam. Store it in a sealed plastic bag to retain the moisture. Once this type of foam dries out, it will not fully absorb moisture again.

Dried flowers
With the right care, you can prolong the decorative life of a dried-flower wreath, garland or swag almost indefinitely.

Many dried flowers are brittle, and need to be handled with care. If flowerheads snap off from the stalks, mount them on wires and bind them with floral tape.

Store dried flowers between layers of tissue paper in boxes, away from the light and where cats and other animals may not be tempted to slumber.

Position dried-flower designs away from strong sunlight, which causes the flowers to fade. It is preferable to hang a wreath, for example, on a south wall beside a window rather than on the wall opposite, where strong shafts of light would strike it.

Keep dried-flower decorations in a dry, airy room. Steamy bathrooms and kitchens are not suitable, as delicate flowers will reabsorb moisture and develop mould.

In these circumstances, when ventilation is poor, choose designs composed of sturdy plant materials such as woody seedpods and stems.

When dried-flower decorations eventually become dusty, take them outside or to a window and simply blow the dust off, or use a hairdryer on the lowest speed. Before doing so, check that all the stems are firmly attached.

If a few of the dried flowers in a design fade, carefully remove them and replace them with more colourful examples.

BOWS
A bow provides the finishing touch to a swag, wreath or garland. There are innumerable materials that are suitable and lots of ways of tying them.

Tying a quick ribbon bow
Even a simple bow can look stunning when a fabulous ribbon is used. Experiment with grosgrain, velvet, satin, taffeta and paper ribbon, as well as lace, net, cord, raffia and rope.

Cut a length of the chosen ribbon and find the centre. Make two equal loops on each side of the centre *(below)*.

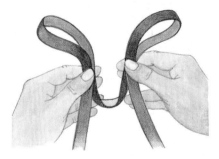

Cross the left-hand loop over the right-hand loop and pull through the centre gap *(below)*. Adjust the loops and trim each end at an angle or into an inverted "V" shape.

Making a one-piece fabric bow

A stylish fabric bow is quick and easy to make when only one piece of fabric is used.

Cut a strip of fabric to a width of twice the desired finished width plus 1¼in (3cm) and a length of the required finished length plus 1¼in (3cm). Fold the strip in half lengthwise with right sides together; pin and stitch along the length, leaving an opening in the centre. Press the seam open and over the centre of the strip. Pin and stitch diagonally across each end (below).

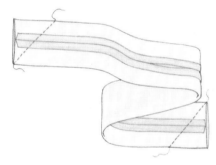

Trim off the triangles at each end, and turn right side out through the centre. Slipstitch the opening closed.

Tie a knot in the centre of the fabric. With the lengthwise seam at the back, thread one end of the fabric strip through the knot. Now thread the other end through the knot. Pull both loops of fabric to form the bow.

Making a wired (French) ribbon bow

Wired (French) ribbon looks wonderful but the wired edges make it difficult to tie. Here is a better way to make a wired ribbon bow.

Cut two lengths of wired ribbon, one four times the length of the desired loop and the other slightly shorter.

Turn in both ends of the longer length to meet in the centre; pin. Fold the second length into loops in the

same way. Place the shorter one centrally over the longer one and tack (baste) in the centre (below).

Cut a short length of unwired ribbon and fold it over the centre; catch the ends together at the back. If desired, you can make tails with a length of wired ribbon, folding it in half and catching it in with the central loop.

STITCHES AND SEAMS

Here are the basic sewing techniques you need for many of the projects in Chapters 3 and 4. If you are left-handed, reverse these instructions.

Tacking (basting)

This is a temporary rather than a permanent stitch, used to hold two materials together while the main (permanent) stitching is worked.

Fasten the end either with a knot or with a couple of small backstitches on the spot. Then take stitches ½in (1.3cm) long through the fabrics.

Once the main stitching is complete, snip off the knot at the end and pull out the tacking stitches.

Running stitch

This stitch is used for gathering or when stitching fine seams by hand. Work from right to left. If you are gathering, make sure that the thread is long enough to complete the area to be gathered.

Begin with a couple of backstitches on the spot then weave the needle in

and out of the fabric with small evenly spaced stitches about ⅛in (3mm) long. The stitches should be approximately the same distance apart as their length.

Fasten off with a couple of backstitches, unless you are gathering. To gather, leave an end of thread for pulling up into gathers (below).

Backstitch

Backstitch imitates a machine stitch, so this is the stitch to use when sewing seams by hand. It is one of the strongest hand stitches, with the stitches overlapping on the underside. Work from right to left.

Begin with a couple of stitches on the spot to secure the thread then work one running stitch and space.

Take the needle back over the space, bringing it out the same distance ahead.

Continue along the seamline, each time inserting the needle in the end of the last stitch and bringing it out one stitch ahead (below).

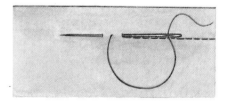

Slipstitch

This is a neat, almost invisible stitch that is used to catch a folded edge in place, such as when using bias binding.

Working from right to left, fasten the thread with a knot hidden inside the folded material. Bring the needle out and pick up a tiny stitch below the folded edge, being careful to pick up only a thread or two.

Run the needle through the folded edge, and bring it out further along. Continue in the same way, making evenly spaced stitches about $1/8$—$1/4$in (3—6mm) apart *(below)*.

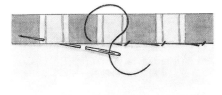

Herringbone stitch (blind catchstitch)

This is a strong hemming stitch which is also used to catch two pieces of wadding (batting) together and to hold non-fusible interfacing in place. Work from left to right, with the needle point always facing to the left.

Secure the thread with a couple of backstitches on the spot, then take a straight stitch in the fabric $1/4$in (6mm) below the hem.

Take the needle diagonally up to the hem and take another straight stitch in the same direction.

Continue in this way, overlapping the ends of the stitches and forming elongated crosses *(below)*.

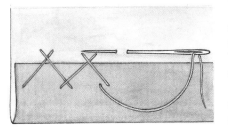

Stitching a plain seam

This is the most common type of seam. Flat, neat and inconspicuous, it has just one row of stitching.

Place the two pieces of fabric with right sides together and raw edges even; pin and tack (baste) $5/8$in (1.5cm) from the edge.

Now machine stitch following the tacking lines, beginning and finishing either by tying the threads securely or by working a few machine stitches in reverse at each end of the seam. Remove the tacking. Finally, press the completed seam open.

If the fabric is bulky, you will probably need to trim the seam allowance to reduce bulk. If both seam allowances are to be turned in the same direction, it's a good idea to trim them to different widths; this is known as layering or grading.

Unless the seam is enclosed it will have to be neatened (finished). Neaten the raw edges by machine zigzag stitch, or cut along the edges with pinking shears, or bind over the edges with bias binding.

When stitching a right-angled corner, stitch into the corner but not beyond it. Then, with the needle in the fabric, raise the foot and turn the fabric 90 degrees; lower the foot and continue to stitch down the next side. After stitching, snip off the corner within the seam allowance. With an inner corner, you should clip into the corner within the seam allowance.

When the corner is very sharp, work one, two or three stitches across the corner, before stitching the next side. Then trim down the fabric well around the point.

On curves, snip into outward curves and cut small notches out of inward curves *(top of next column)*. This will

help the fabric to lie flat. Be very careful not to snip through the stitching.

BIAS BINDING

Bias binding is a neat way of finishing a raw edge as well as adding a touch of colour or pattern. Although you can buy bias binding, making your own gives you more choice in terms of fabric and width.

Making your own binding

Decide on the width of the binding and multiply by four. Fold over the corner of the fabric to meet the cut edge. Cut through the diagonal fold then cut strips to the desired width, with the edges parallel to this. Join the ends of these bias strips on the straight grain *(below)*, until you have a continuous strip of binding to the desired length.

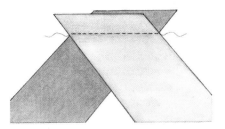

Now either press in each side of the bias binding by one quarter or pass the strip through a commercial tape-and-binding maker, pressing the binding as it comes out neatly folded.

Binding an edge

To bind the edge of a piece of fabric, unfold one edge of the binding and lay it against the fabric with right sides together and with the crease of the binding along the seamline. Pin and stitch in the crease. Trim the fabric if necessary and fold the binding over the edge to the opposite side. Pin and slipstitch the binding in place over the previous stitches *(below)*; or, if it is to be topstitched, bring the binding over the raw edge, pin and stitch.

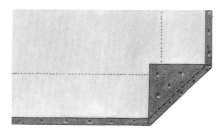

MITRING CORNERS

Mitring eliminates bulk so that corners are neat and flat. There are various methods of mitring.

Mitring a turned-in edge

Use this method to trim away excess fabric so your turned-in edge has flat, smooth corners.

On a single hem, press under ¹/₄in (6mm). Turn up the hem to the required length and press. Unfold and turn in the corner diagonally so that the diagonal fold meets the hem fold; press. Mark a line ¹/₄in (6mm) from the diagonal fold *(below)*.

Trim off the corner along the marked line. Refold the hem over the trimmed corner *(below)*.

Mitring a flat trimming

This mitre is done while you are attaching a flat trimming such as ribbon or braid.

Place the trim against the fabric edge; pin and stitch in place up to the corner and fasten off. Fold the trimming back on itself, with the fold matching the next edge; pin firmly.

Turn down the trimming along the next edge, pressing the diagonal fold that forms across the corner. Lift the trimming and stitch across the diagonal crease. Trim off the excess fabric across the corner *(below)*.

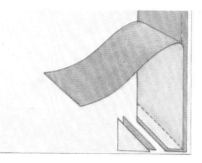

Now replace the trimming and continue stitching along the next edge. When all the corners have been mitred in the same way, stitch around the trimming along the inside edge *(top of next column)*.

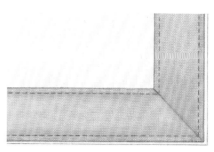

Mitring binding

When you are applying bias binding, you may have to apply it around an outward corner. Here is how to mitre the corner as neatly as possible.

Unfold one of the prefolded edges of the bias binding and place it against the edge of the fabric. Pin and machine stitch in the crease of the binding up to the seamline of the next edge, and then fasten off the threads securely.

Fold the binding diagonally away from the fabric, aligning the edge of the binding with the fabric edge that you will be binding next. Pin and stitch again, beginning the stitching at the edge *(below)*.

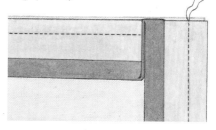

Take the binding over the raw edge to the opposite side of the fabric, folding the excess fabric into a neat mitre. On the wrong side of the fabric, tuck under the excess binding to form a neat mitre here too.

Pin and slipstitch the remaining folded edge of binding in place, stitching across the mitre on each side only when the binding is wide.

GLOSSARY

American readers may not be familiar with some of the following terms.

British	American
broderie anglais	teyelet
cling-film	plastic wrap
craft knife	X-Acto or mat knife
florist's stub wire	florist's wire, 18-guage
fray	travel
frill	truffle
gypsophila	baby's breath
haberdashery department/store	notions department/store
herringbone stitch	blind catchstitch
hessian	burlap
neaten edges	finish edges
oversew	overcast
plait	braid
PVA glue	craft or white glue
reel wire	spool wire or paddle wire
tacking	basting
wadding	batting

SOURCES OF SUPPLY

* denotes mail-order availability

CRAFT SUPPLIES

Fred Aldous Ltd *
PO Box 135, 37 Lever St, Manchester M60 1UX,
England
Tel 0661-236 2477

The Handicraft Shop *
47 Northgate, Canterbury CT1 1BE, England
Tel 01227-451188

Pastimes *
9 & 11 Power St, Kings Lynn, Norfolk PE30 1EJ,
England
Tel 01553-762907

Beadworks *
139 Washington St, South Norwalk, CT 06854,
USA

Enterprise Art *
PO Box 2918, Largo, FL 34649, USA

Sax Arts & Crafts *
PO Box 51710, New Berlin, WI 53153, USA

Camden Art Centre Pty Ltd *
188-200 Gertrude St, Fitzroy, Victoria 3065,
Australia

Janet's Art Supplies
145 Victoria Ave, Chatswood, NSW 2057,
Australia

Queensland Handicrafts
6 Manning St, South Brisbane, Queensland
4101, Australia
Tel 07-844 5722

FABRICS AND SEWING SUPPLIES

Borovick Fabrics Ltd *
16 Berwick St, London W1V 4HP, England
Tel 0171-4372180

Calico Corners
Wayne, PA 19087, USA
Tel 215-688 1505
or 1-800-821 7700 ext 810 for nearest retail
outlet

Clotilde, Inc *
Box 22312, Fort Lauderdale, FL 33315-2312,
USA
Tel 1-800 772 2891

Nancy's Notions *
PO Box 683, Beaver Dam, WI 53916-0683, USA
Tel 1-800-765 0690
or 414-887 0391 for catalog

U-Do Haberdashery & Craft
Shop 16, North Gate Centre, Glenorchy,
Tasmania, Australia
Tel 002-73 1220

TRIMMINGS

Hamilworth Ltd *
23 Lime Rd, Dumbarton G82 2RP, Scotland
Tel 01389-32783
(flowermaking stamens, wires, tapes)

V V Rouleaux *
10 Symons St, London SW3 8TJ, England
Tel 0171-7304413

M & J Trimmings
1008 Sixth Ave, New York, NY 10018, USA
Tel 212-391 9072

The Ribbon Outlet, Inc
Tel 1-800-766 BOWS for nearest retail outlet

FLOWER ARRANGERS' SUNDRIES

The Diddybox *
132/134 Belmont Rd, Astley Bridge, Bolton,
Lancs BL1 7AN, England
Tel 01204-592 405

Simply Garlands *
51 Albion Road, Pitstone, Beds LU7 9AY,
England
Tel 01296-661425
(mechanics for garlands)

C B Enterprises *
26002-B Marguerite Parkway, Suite 412,
Mission Viejo, CA 92692, USA
(wreath decor)

Robert Moffit *
PO Box 3597, Wilmington, DE 19807, USA
(flower-preserving crystals)

DRIED FLOWERS AND SEEDHEADS

Norpar Flowers *
Navestock Hall, Navestock, Essex RM4 1HA,
England
Tel 01277-374968

INDEX

ACKNOWLEDGEMENTS
The authors would like to thank the following for their help: **Penny Hill** and **Beryl Miller** for their help with projects in the third and fourth chapters. **Norpar Flowers**, Navestock, Essex, England for supplying all the dried flowers and many of the dried seedheads. **Panda Ribbons**, Selectus Ltd, Stoke on Trent, England, for all the ribbons used in the third and fourth chapters, which are available from good haberdashery departments. **Simply Garlands**, Pitstone, Bedfordshire, England, for supplying the garland cores.

The pictures on the following pages are by: Patrice de Villiers pages 8/9, 10, 12/13; Shona Wood pages 13, 14; Di Lewis page 15; Andreas von Einsiedel (reproduced courtesy of Elizabeth Whiting Associates) page 11 top; Di Lewis (reproduced courtesy of Elizabeth Whiting Associates) page 11, bottom.